Was Yosef on the Spectrum?

Was Yosef on the Spectrum?

Understanding Joseph

Through Torah, Midrash, and Classical Jewish Sources

SAMUEL J. LEVINE

URIM PUBLICATIONS
Jerusalem • New York

Was Yosef on the Spectrum? Understanding Joseph Through Torah, Midrash, and Classical Jewish Sources
Samuel J. Levine

Printed in Israel

First Edition

ISBN 9781602803220

Urim Publications
P.O. Box 52287
Jerusalem 9152102
Israel

www.UrimPublications.com

Library of Congress Cataloging-in-Publication Data in progress.

Names: Levine, Samuel J., author.
Title: Was Yosef on the spectrum? : understanding Joseph through Torah, midrash, and classical Jewish sources / Samuel J. Levine.
Description: First Edition. | Jerusalem ; New York : Urim Publications, [2019]
Identifiers: LCCN 2018037070 | ISBN 9781602803220 (hardcover : alk. paper)
Subjects: LCSH: Joseph (Son of Jacob) | Joseph, Son of Jacob—In rabbinical literature. | Bible. Genesis, XXXVII–XLIV—Commentaries. | Autism in literature.
Classification: LCC BS580.J6 L487 2018 | DDC 222/.11092—dc23
LC record available at https://lccn.loc.gov/2018037070

"Prof. Levine is both a *ben Torah* and an accomplished scholar. His work is an act of both courage and love of Yosef. Courage – because some will criticize him for trying to diminish the stature of one of the *shivah ro'im*, when his intention was the very opposite. Love – because in order to address the difficulties many have raised with aspects of Yosef's behavior, he worked thoroughly and painstakingly with traditional sources to advance his theory, rather than ignore them as so many others do. Whether the reader accepts Prof. Levine's thesis or remains skeptical (as I do), we must imagine Yosef smiling at someone who labored so hard to defend him."

– Rabbi Yitzchok Adlerstein,
author of *Nesivos Shalom*

"Levine's interpretation of Yosef's life through the lens of contemporary psychology is innovative and provides a way for readers to find personal and practical insights for how to approach neurodiversity in the Jewish community today. While the topic is potentially controversial, Levine treats it with scholarship and respect and comes up with a very strong reading of the narrative. It is an interesting take and a worthwhile read."

– Rabbi Dr. Ira Bedzow,
Director of Biomedical Ethics and Humanities,
NY Medical College

"Sam Levine was my student in yeshiva, and I have known him for decades as he has continued to study and teach Jewish law. I enjoyed his book on Yosef, which presents a thoughtful and creative literary analysis of the story, based on a close reading of the Chumash, *midrashim*, and classical *meforshim*."

– Rav Menachem Mendel Blachman,
Senior Ra"m at Yeshivat Kerem B'Yavneh

"Sam Levine has created a fresh, thoughtful and new perspective on a classic story, offering readers a unique lens with which to view one of Genesis's most colorful characters. In the process, he sensitizes us to what it means to live and lead on the spectrum, turning a handicap into a ladder for incredible future triumph for Joseph and for all those who come after him who struggle yet succeed."

– Dr. Erica Brown,
author of *Jonah: The Reluctant Prophet*

"As he lays out his extraordinarily bold, profoundly thought-provoking hypothesis, Levine's deep love for and highly nuanced understanding of his subject leaps from every page."

– George Rohr,
noted philanthropist

"Levine presents a compelling portrait of Yosef, based on a close and insightful reading of the biblical text and traditional Jewish sources. As Levine describes in careful detail, individuals on the autism spectrum often possess a powerful set of strengths and abilities, and provide both countless tangible and intangible benefits to society. A sensitive reader will never look at Yosef, or individuals with autism, in the same way again.

More broadly, this book will spark conversation and awareness, and hopefully change attitudes toward individuals with disabilities, both within the Jewish community and beyond."

– Jay Ruderman,
President of the Ruderman Family Foundation

"This work represents a deeply researched close reading of the story of Yosef. Readers will experience a thought provoking analysis of Yosef's personality and a window into the lives of those on the highly functioning end of the autistic spectrum and their families. Recommended reading!"

– Dr. Deena Zimmerman,
author of *A Lifetime Companion to the Laws of Jewish Family Life*

Contents

Introduction

THE STORY OF YOSEF (JOSEPH) presents some of the most challenging questions of all biblical narratives. Yosef's behavior, interpersonal relationships, and personal journey and development are often difficult to understand, and at times seem to defy explanation. Leading commentators are repeatedly puzzled both by Yosef's actions and by the events that surround him: from Yosef's bitter interchanges with his brothers, which his father Yaakov (Jacob) is apparently unable to mediate, to the events in the Land of Egypt, where Yosef finds both failure and remarkable success, to Yosef's strange machinations, when his brothers travel to Egypt to purchase food and later settle in Egypt along with Yaakov.

Commentators have offered a variety of approaches in an effort to understand and explain many of these difficulties. Yet, these explanations tend to be incomplete, often responding to individual events and aspects of the story, without providing a cohesive understanding of the story as a whole and the puzzling ways Yosef interacts with others. Moreover, although commentators sometimes find common ground in their views of certain episodes, their approaches often contradict one another, and at times their interpretations of different events seem inherently inconsistent.

This book attempts to achieve a coherent and cohesive reading of the story that offers a plausible understanding of Yosef's behaviors toward others and those of others toward him, while at the same time accounting for both his successes and his failures. Toward that goal, the book suggests that a close reading of the biblical text paints a portrait of Yosef consistent with an individual on the autism spectrum.[1]

Although individuals with autism spectrum disorders vary widely in their symptoms and their behaviors, common characteristics include many of the behaviors Yosef exhibits and the interactions he experiences, such as: social challenges, punctuated by an inability to read social cues, understand and anticipate the feelings and reactions of others, and navigate social settings; attachment to animals or to inanimate objects in place of interpersonal relationships; heightened intellectual capacity and creativity in narrow areas of interest; repetitive and inflexible behaviors; an obsessive and compulsive focus on a private way of perceiving the world; and a rigid and literal perspective on truth, ethics, and morality that sees virtue in extreme terms rather than allowing for nuance.

In addition to offering a way to understand Yosef's behaviors and interactions, picturing Yosef as an individual on the autism spectrum, moving from childhood through his adult life and career, provides continuity to the remarkably varied experi-

---

1. This project does not aim to categorize – let alone diagnose – Yosef with any degree of clinical precision. Indeed, the thesis of this project is premised on the notion that the portrait of Yosef presented in the text of the Torah is intended for the close, careful, and sensitive reader, not for the clinician. Accordingly, the project relies on a close textual reading and the insights of leading biblical interpreters, spanning thousands of years and geographical locations across the world, who applied their non-clinical wisdom, experience, and powers of observation. Based on these sources and analyses, it may be helpful for contemporary readers to observe that Yosef's behaviors and experiences closely resemble many of those common among individuals with forms of high-functioning autism or Asperger's syndrome. For clinical descriptions and diagnostic criteria, see, e.g., *Diagnostic and Statistical Manual of Mental Disorders (DSM–5): Autism Spectrum Disorder; Social (Pragmatic) Communication Disorder; Diagnostic and Statistical Manual of Mental Disorders (DSM-IV): Autistic Disorder; Asperger's Disorder.*

It should also be emphasized that this portrait of Yosef is not a simplistic and ahistorical labeling based on a superficial reading of a few events recorded thousands of years ago, but instead represents a carefully documented understanding of Yosef, based on dozens of statements in the biblical text and hundreds of comments in classical Jewish sources including *midrashim*, *rishonim*, and *acharonim*.

ences Yosef undergoes at different stages of the story. Viewed through this lens, Yosef emerges as a more familiar and less enigmatic individual, exhibiting both strengths and weaknesses commonly associated with autism spectrum disorder, facing concomitant and interconnected challenges and opportunities, and experiencing, often at once, both surprising success and unexpected failure.[2]

Perhaps most importantly, understanding Yosef as an individual on the spectrum helps illuminate not only the text of the Torah on a *p'shat* level (plain reading),[3] but also many comments and teachings about Yosef found in classical Jewish sources, including *midrashim, rishonim,* and *acharonim.* To be sure, none of these sources contains a comprehensive depiction of Yosef that would fully comport with contemporary understandings of autism spectrum disorder. However, a close reading of many of the classical sources suggests that for thousands of years, leading scholars have presented insights and explanations producing a portrait of Yosef consistent with a person who exhibits a number of characteristics and behaviors associated with contemporary views of the autism spectrum. Thus, applying contemporary psychological insights serves as a way to remain faithful to traditional interpretations while at the

2. It should go without saying, but may need to be noted, that this way of analyzing the story of Yosef should not be seen as casting Yosef in a negative light. Instead, this project is an effort to understand Yosef, on a human level and through a reading that is faithful to the *p'shat* of the text of the Torah, similar to the way nearly all of the classical and authoritative *midrashim, rishonim,* and *acharonim* work to understand the story. Cf. *Minchas Asher,* Bereishis 561 note*. If anything, compared with the highly critical interpretations often found in many of these sources, seeing Yosef as an individual on the spectrum tends to render both Yosef and those who interact with him less susceptible to criticism and more open to sympathy and understanding. Most basically, being on the spectrum is not a moral vice, and the condition of autism spectrum disorder does not invite or imply a reason or avenue for criticism.

3. The particularly high degree of difficulty in explaining the story of Yosef on a *p'shat* level may have served as the motivation for the extended – and otherwise, unusually placed – disquisition by Rashbam, at the start of the story, describing his methodology of focusing on the *p'shat* of the text. See Rashbam 37:2.

same time bringing together many of these different approaches to provide a more unified and complete picture of Yosef.[4]

Finally, although the primary goal of this project is focused on exploring a way to understand the character of Yosef and the events that surround him, with this understanding, the story may offer lessons for interactions with children and adults on the spectrum. If so, the fact that upon a close and careful reading the Torah contains such lessons, which are both current and timeless, is a further illustration of the principle: *hafoch bah, v'hafoch bah, d'kula bah* ("turn it and turn it, for everything is in it").[5]

4. Accordingly, applying a method often utilized by scholars in the context of both *halacha* and *aggada*, this project aims to present a fresh approach that relies on disparate strands of traditional and highly authoritative sources of interpretation, while at the same time acknowledging that none of the earlier sources expressly or entirely adopts the new approach. Cf. Rabbi Aharon Lichtenstein, *Leaves of Faith: The World of Jewish Learning* 78–79; Rabbi Hershel Schachter, *B'Ikvei Hatzoan* 1–3; Rabbi Yosef Dov Soloveitchik, *Ra'ayonot al haTefillah* 1–2, in *Ish haHalacha – Galuy V'nistar* 239–40.

5. Mishna, Avot 5:25.

Chapter 1

Yosef and His Brothers: *Ro'eh et Echav* and *Na'ar*

> These are the generations of Yaakov: Yosef, at the age of seventeen, was a shepherd, with his brothers, of the flocks [*ro'eh et echav batzoan*], and he was a child [*na'ar*] with the sons of Bilhah and with the sons of Zilpah, his father's wives, and Yosef brought bad reports of them to their father.[1]

A close reading of the initial depictions of Yosef and his interactions with his brothers and his father reveals a number of characteristics common to a child on the autism spectrum. Yosef is first introduced as seventeen years old and *ro'eh et echav batzoan.*[2] Several commentators interpret this phrase to indicate that, although he was only seventeen years old and younger than his brothers, in his role as a shepherd, Yosef was their leader and their guide. He used his superior knowledge and understanding of the needs of sheep to teach his brothers the skills required of a shepherd.[3]

It is not uncommon for children on the spectrum to feel a special connection to animals, at times feeling more comfortable and at ease with animals than with people. As a result, animals may be provided to children on the spectrum to facilitate forms of therapy and relaxation. In fact, individuals on the spectrum are often more adept, and accordingly more successful, when

1. 37:2. Unless otherwise noted, references are to chapter and verse in Sefer Bereishis (The Book of Genesis). All translations are the author's.
2. 37:2
3. See, e.g., Abravanel; Sforno 37:2; *HaK'sav V'haKabbala* 37:2.

working with animals or with inanimate objects, such as cars or technology, than they are when working with people. In contrast to his inability to interact with or relate to his brothers on a social level, to a degree that they found it impossible even to tolerate him,[4] Yosef displayed such skill and talent relating to animals that his brothers could not deny his expertise and were compelled to accept his leadership.

In the next phrase, Yosef is described as "a *na'ar* with the sons of Bilhah and with the sons of Zilpah."[5] *Midrash Rabbah* points out the incongruity of referring to Yosef as a *na'ar*, a term ordinarily reserved for a young child, when the same verse previously stated that he was seventeen years old.[6] The midrash, as cited by Rashi, explains that Yosef is deemed a *na'ar* because he engages in childish activities, such as fixing his hair and tending to his eyes.[7] However, although Rashi cites only these two behaviors, the midrash also enumerates a third behavior, which in some way involves lifting his heels.[8] Notably, playing with one's eyes, twirling one's hair, and kicking one's heels are all forms of self-stimulatory and repetitive behaviors that are unusual for a typical seventeen-year-old child, but common behaviors for a child on the spectrum.

In fact, unlike Rashi's explanation, not found in the midrash, that Yosef engaged in these behaviors to look nice,[9] *Midrash Lekach Tov* adds that Yosef was *mitga'ga* (enjoyed himself)

4. See 37:4.

5. 37:2.

6. See *Torah Shelema* 37:2 [33]. References follow the citation form that is used in *Torah Shelema*, corresponding to the bracketed numerals that precede the text and the notes, respectively.

As Ramban observes, Yosef was not much younger than many of his brothers – possibly just a year or two their junior. See Ramban 37:3. If so, the characterization of Yosef as a *na'ar* would seem to carry an additional meaning beyond an allusion to his age. According to Ramban, however, the word *na'ar* simply reflects that Yosef was younger than the sons of Bilhah and Zilpah, who usually accompanied him. See Ramban 37:2.

7. See Rashi 37:2.

8. See *Torah Shelema* [33]. The midrash uses the phrase, *m'taleh b'akevo*, perhaps evoking toe walking, a common behavior among children on the spectrum. See also *Torah Shelema* note [33].

9. See Rashi 37:2.

through these activities.[10] Thus, rather than suggesting that these actions were directed towards others in an effort to improve his appearance, the midrash attributes to Yosef a kind of self-enjoyment,[11] consistent with the self-stimulatory satisfaction that children on the spectrum achieve from similar behaviors.

Evidently as a result of these characteristics, which may be representative of other characteristics and behaviors indicative of autism spectrum disorder, Yosef has already experienced social difficulties with his brothers. Indeed, Yosef appears together with the children of Bilhah and Zilpah, even though his own mother, Rachel, has the same status as Leah. According to Rashi, Yosef has been ostracized and marginalized by the sons of Leah, leading him to seek the companionship of his less prominent brothers.[12] Yet, even in a setting with peers who might be expected to be more accepting of Yosef and less likely to disapprove of his characteristics and behaviors, Yosef has trouble navigating his social environment.

Pursuant to some kind of conflict, Yosef approaches his father Yaakov and tells him about the brothers' wrongful words or actions.[13] The text does not recount the substance or nature of Yosef's remarks about his brothers, or even identify which brothers' conduct has prompted him to approach Yaakov. While commentators provide a range of explanations, often differing substantially, to flesh out these details, nearly any understanding of this episode yields a clear illustration of Yosef's continuing social difficulties with his peers and his need to seek adult attention and protection, both common qualities among children on the autism spectrum.

For example, according to Radak, Yosef told his father about his brothers' expressions of hatred toward him, which he expe-

---

10. See *Torah Shelema* note [33]. This midrash cites Yosef's behaviors relating to his hair and his heels.

11. Based on the Targum to Psalms 119:117, the Jastrow Dictionary offers the translation "to enjoy one's self" for the similar word, *iga'ga*.

12. See Rashi 37:2. Although some commentators suggest that Yosef was admirably humble in associating with the sons of Bilhah and Zilpah, see Abravanel; *HaK'sav V'haKabbala* 37:2, these commentators likewise recognize that it is surprising to find Yosef with this group of brothers.

13. 37:2.

rienced at the hands of both the sons of Leah and the sons of Bilhah and Zilpah.[14] Significantly, Radak offers different motivations for the hatred each of these groups directed toward Yosef, corresponding to the distinct nature of each group's separate interactions with him.[15] Children on the spectrum may be the target of hostility from different segments of their peer groups, including both popular children with an elevated social status, like the sons of Leah, and sometimes just as likely, children who are themselves relegated to a lower social status, like the sons of Bilhah and Zilpah. Unable to respond to this hostility in a socially appropriate manner, children on the spectrum often find that their only recourse is to turn immediately to an authority figure, a teacher or a parent, as Yosef turned to Yaakov, with the desperate and usually misguided hope that reporting on their peers will resolve the situation.

Other commentators, following the midrash, suggest that Yosef told Yaakov about various other forms of improper conduct, unrelated to himself, which he witnessed among his brothers.[16] At the same time, these commentators emphasize that Yosef did not fabricate the information he provided Yaakov, nor did he intend to embarrass his brothers. Rather, Yosef accurately reported his brothers' conduct and spoke only to Yaakov, with the aim that their father, once aware of their misdeeds, would bring them back to the proper path.[17] Nevertheless, despite Yosef's good intentions, telling his father about his brothers' improper conduct would lead to further repercussions for himself. The midrash, cited by Rashi, directly correlates Yosef's statements about his brothers with various misfortunes Yosef would later suffer at the hands of both the brothers and others he would encounter.[18]

14. See Radak 37:2. *HaK'sav V'haKabbala* interprets the word *dibah* in this verse to denote hatred, while offering a different understanding of the meaning of the verse and the course of events in this episode. See *HaK'sav V'haKabbala* 37:2.

15. Ramban and Chizkuni likewise offer different motivations for each group's hatred of Yosef. See Ramban 37:2; Chizkuni 37:2.

16. See *Torah Shelema* [36]; Rashi 37:2; Abravanel; Sforno 37:2.

17. See Abravanel, *HaK'sav V'haKabbala* 37:2.

18. See *Torah Shelema* [37]; Rashi 37:2.

Commentators query why, according to the midrash, Yosef was punished for conveying accurate – albeit negative – information for the limited purpose of helping correct his brothers' wrongful ways.[19] Although a number of answers have been offered,[20] on both a human level and a *p'shat* level[21] Yosef's error is obvious. As Sforno and Maharal observe, in telling his father about his brothers' misconduct, Yosef acted like a *na'ar*, a young child who, because of his inexperience, is unable to anticipate the ramifications of his actions.[22] Surely, Yosef should have realized that telling on his brothers would only antagonize them further, exacerbate his alienation from them,[23] and possibly even result in danger to himself. Indeed, the brothers' hatred toward Yosef continues to grow until they ultimately throw him in a pit and sell him.[24] In this context, the midrash understandably correlates Yosef's accusations about his brothers with the violence they would later perpetrate against him.[25]

Thus, Yosef's interactions with his brothers are again consistent with a number of characteristics and experiences often associated with individuals on the spectrum. The childish – and childlike – quality Sforno and Maharal identify, in Yosef's failure to consider the consequences of his actions, seems to reflect a broader impulsivity and lack of self-restraint on Yosef's part. At the age of seventeen, Yosef should have developed the self-control necessary to avoid acting in ways that would later cause harm to himself. Instead, his disability prevents him from thinking about the future, and his inability to rein in his

---

19. See Mizrachi 37:2; *Gur Aryeh* 37:2.

20. See, e.g., Mizrachi 37:2.

21. Although some commentators question why the *midrashim* interpret this verse in a way that portrays Yosef in a negative light, see *Torah Shelema* note [36], on a *p'shat* level, the text can be readily understood as critical of Yosef.

22. See Sforno 37:2; *Gur Aryeh* 37:2. See also Chizkuni 37:2; *Meleches Machsheves* 37:2.

23. According to Ramban and Chizkuni, while the sons of Leah had other reasons for hating Yosef, the sons of Bilhah and Zilpah began to hate him because he reported on them to Yaakov. See Ramban 37:2; Chizkuni 37:2.

24. See 37:24, 28.

25. See *Torah Shelema* [37].

impulses and desires will ultimately prove highly detrimental to him.

Alternatively, Sforno and Maharal may be highlighting Yosef's lack of attention to, and awareness of, the feelings of others, and concomitantly, Yosef's inability to anticipate the reactions others will have toward him. Like many individuals on the spectrum, Yosef is focused intently on his own perceptions and perspectives of the people and the world around him, relatively – if not largely – oblivious to the way others see him.[26] While it seems obvious to the detached observer that informing on his brothers will only breed further animosity on their part, Yosef is absorbed in his own world[27] and acts without taking into account how his actions will be perceived and the feelings they will engender.[28]

In either event, Yosef's determination to tell his father of his brothers' wrongdoing, notwithstanding the negative ramifications for his own well-being, may exemplify another central aspect of Yosef's character common for an individual on the spectrum. Yosef has a close connection to truth and a powerful commitment to morality, leading to a compulsion to express his views, often in stark terms, regardless of other considerations. Thus, like many on the spectrum, in scenarios that call

26. This quality of Yosef may account for the Talmud's statement that *ayin hara* does not affect Yosef's lineage. See Talmud Bavli, Berachot 20a. Rabbi Yosef Dov Soloveitchik suggests that because *ayin hara* depends on the way others see a person, it does not affect Yosef, since he remained true to his ethical principles regardless of how others viewed him. See Rabbi Hershel Schachter, *Nefesh Harav* 63–66 (citing Rabbi Yosef Dov Soloveitchik, *Divrei Hashkafa* 199–201).

Yet, this suggestion may not fully explain why Yosef was singled out in this regard, as surely other figures, in the Torah, in *Nach*, and at many other times in Jewish history, demonstrated a similar faithfulness to their principles in the face of challenges and opposition. Taking Rabbi Soloveitchik's approach one step further, perhaps Yosef differed in that, beyond not caring, Yosef did not even realize what others thought of him, thus completely negating the possibility of *ayin hara*.

27. Indeed, as Rav Dessler explains, the Torah and Talmud compare Yosef to fish, in part because "they live as if they are in another world." See *Michtav M'Eliyahu* 4:6.

28. Rav Dessler develops, at some length, a similar understanding of Yosef's character and behaviors. See *Michtav M'Eliyahu* 2:227–29.

for diplomacy or discretion, Yosef bluntly speaks the truth as he sees it, even to his own detriment. Though his brothers have engaged in wrongful activities, there does not seem to be an urgent need to immediately inform Yaakov, particularly when those activities are not directed at Yosef.[29] Accordingly, Yosef's failure to recognize and comply with social mores compounds his earlier social challenges and leads to further conflict with his brothers.

Maharal offers yet another interpretation of the midrash, suggesting that although the brothers' actions may have resembled wrongful conduct, they did not technically violate any prohibitions. Nevertheless, because Yosef was a *tzadik gamur* (completely righteous), he viewed their conduct as sinful, and therefore found it necessary to report them as such to his father.[30] Under this interpretation, Yosef's tendency to exhibit autistic-like behaviors becomes even more striking.

Like many on the spectrum, Yosef sees the world in black and white, unable to appreciate – or tolerate – nuance, both in his approach to morality and in the way he responds and interacts with those around him. Yosef perceives and characterizes any deviation from truth as a manifestation of wrongdoing, and he feels compelled to share his perceptions of truth with others, in extreme and categorical terms.[31] If the brothers did not, in fact, commit these sins, they likely found Yosef's accusations both inexplicable and infuriating. Just as Yosef is unable to understand how his actions are perceived by others, his brothers are unable to understand Yosef, finding him puzzling, annoying, and possibly even threatening.[32]

---

29. The language Rashi employs may be notable in this regard. Rashi writes that "every misdeed he observed in his brothers, the sons of Leah, he brought to his father," Rashi 37:2, possibly indicating Yosef's inner compulsion to inform his father of each and every misdeed, including those not directly affecting Yosef.

30. See *Gur Aryeh* 37:2.

31. Cf. *Michtav M'Eliyahu* 2:228–29.

32. Cf. *Gur Aryeh* 37:2 (Yosef's brothers hated him and wanted to kill him because he had a separate and distinct quality); Abravanel 49:22 (interpreting Yaakov's later characterization of Yosef as "different in nature from his brothers" in a way that prompts their jealousy). See also Sforno 37:18.

Chapter 2

Yosef and Yaakov: *Ben Zekunim*

> And Yisrael (Israel) loved Yosef more than all of his [other] sons, because he was a son of his old age [*ben zekunim*], and he made him a fine woolen coat. And his brothers saw that their father loved him more than all of his brothers, and they hated him, and they could not speak with him peaceably.[1]

In light of later events and subsequent descriptions of Yosef, interpreting the term *na'ar*[2] to reflect a degree of immaturity or lack of wisdom raises further questions of its own. For example, as Sforno notes, in contrast to his seeming inability to anticipate the ramifications of his behaviors, Yosef will ultimately emerge as particularly wise when he attains roles of leadership in Egypt,[3] demonstrating a remarkable ability to effectively foresee – and forecast – the future consequences of present actions.[4]

Moreover, the next verse states that of all his sons, Yaakov loved Yosef, because Yosef was a *ben zekunim* to Yaakov.[5] Although some commentators interpret this phrase to refer to Yaakov's advanced age at the time of Yosef's birth,[6] others observe that all of the brothers were born during Yaakov's old

1. 37:3–4.
2. 37:2.
3. See Sforno 37:2.
4. Acknowledging this apparent contradiction, Sforno seems to attribute Yosef's youthful indiscretions to a lack of experience and perspective. See Sforno 37:2.
5. 37:3.
6. See Saadia Gaon 37:3; Rashi 37:3; Ibn Ezra 37:3. See also Rashbam 37:3 (explaining that for many years, Yosef was the youngest son).

age,[7] some just a year or two prior to Yosef,[8] while Binyamin (Benjamin) was born ever later.[9] Instead, following Onkelos, Radak and Ramban understand *ben zekunim* to connote the wisdom that Yaakov found in Yosef, resembling someone of more advanced years.[10] As Abravanel notes, however, depictions of Yosef as possessing wisdom beyond his years seem to directly contradict the description of Yosef as a childish *na'ar*.[11]

Though various resolutions may be offered to these apparent contradictions, the inconsistencies in Yosef's character again evidence qualities of a child on the autism spectrum. It is quite common for children on the spectrum to possess advanced cognitive abilities, but at the same time to engage in behaviors that appear childish, immature, and socially inappropriate, leading them to be marginalized and ostracized by others. Thus, Maharal's portrayal of Yosef, as a *na'ar* who is unsuccessful in his social interactions because of his failure to anticipate how he will be perceived by others and how they will react to him,[12] need not contradict or preclude Yosef's cognitive ability to predict, often with great skill, future trends in other areas.[13]

In addition, children on the spectrum often exhibit inappro-

---

7. See Radak 37:3, Ramban 37:3.
8. See Ramban 37:3.
9. See Chizkuni 37:3. See also Rashbam 37:3.
10. See Onkelos 37:3; Radak 37:3; Ramban 37:3. See also Abravanel.
11. See Abravanel 37:1, Question 3.
12. See *Gur Aryeh* 37:2.
13. Rav Dessler similarly considers, at length, a number of interpretations of the word *na'ar* that at first glance seem contradictory, but which he explains to reflect different strengths and deficits that were present in Yosef at the same time. See *Michtav M'Eliyahu* 2:227–29.

This supposed inconsistency may likewise account for the seemingly incongruent juxtaposition of the description of Yosef as *ro'eh et echav batzoan*, which many commentators interpret as an indication of his shepherding leadership skills, with the description of Yosef as a *na'ar*, who provokes negative interactions with his brothers. 37:2–4. Apparently prompted by this incongruity, Radak suggests that the text uses the word *batzoan* in place of *hatzoan* to connote that Yosef was learning the skills of shepherding along with his brothers. See Radak 37:2. Alternatively, however, the different aspects of Yosef's personality, including both social deficits and skillful shepherding, are not inherently contradictory, and are instead consistent with autism spectrum disorder.

priate social behaviors primarily when they are with their peers, while they maintain – or appear to maintain – a more mature, adult-like, and even wise persona when they encounter adults. Accordingly, it need not prove contradictory – or even surprising – that Yosef is depicted as an immature *na'ar* when pictured with his brothers but as a wise *ben zekunim* when with his father.

Indeed, Ramban emphasizes that the text does not describe Yosef as a *ben zekunim* generally, but only "to [Yaakov]," because he was wise in Yaakov's eyes.[14] Similarly, the text does not refer to Yosef as a *na'ar* generally, but only "with the sons of Bilhah and with the sons of Zilpah."[15] Like many children on the spectrum, Yosef is most susceptible to acting like a *na'ar* when he is with his peers, and seemingly paradoxically, especially when he is with the sons of Bilhah and Zilpah, who are likely the less mature of his brothers. Adults are often able and willing to accommodate, compensate for, and ignore the social missteps of a child on the spectrum – at times on a subconscious level – in part because they recognize, appreciate, and may be overly impressed, or even misled, by the child's advanced skills in other areas. In contrast, peers typically focus on a child's failure to interact with them in a socially appropriate manner, and their hostility may be further exacerbated by a combination of the child's superior cognitive abilities and interests, coupled with their own social challenges and immaturity.

Common for a child on the spectrum, the uneven and unusual nature of Yosef's character makes it particularly difficult for both his peers and his father to fully understand him, prompting them to interact with him in correspondingly uneven and unhelpful ways. Out of his love for Yosef,[16] Yaakov attempts to resolve the conflicts that have arisen between Yosef and his brothers by accommodating Yosef with special treatment. In an apparent effort to bolster Yosef's status in his brothers'

14. See Ramban 37:3.

15. 37:2. Abravanel notes the parallel qualifiers in these verses, though based on his interpretation of *na'ar* as reflecting positively on Yosef, Abravanel understands the verses to emphasize that Yosef acted appropriately and wisely, in separate contexts, with both his father and his brothers. See Abravanel.

16. 37:3.

eyes, Yaakov gives Yosef a special coat or garment[17] that sets Yosef apart from his brothers[18] and establishes his leadership.[19] The description of the garment, as *passim*, is open to various interpretations, including Chizkuni's suggestion that it was an elegant coat, intended *l'phayso* (to appease him),[20] possibly indicating an attempt by Yaakov to indulge Yosef by showing him extra love and attention. Other commentators interpret *passim* as denoting the garment's special colors or fabric,[21] possibly intended to highlight Yosef's unique personality and special talents.[22]

Whatever his goal, Yaakov does not bring about his intended results; quite to the contrary, Yaakov's actions further amplify the troubles Yosef experiences with his peers. Rather than following Yaakov's lead in showing extra regard for Yosef, when the brothers see that Yaakov loves him the most, they respond with outright hatred of Yosef.[23] Yaakov seems to have taken the first of several missteps in his parenting of Yosef, and in fact, the Talmud, midrash, and Rambam cite Yaakov's error as a cautionary tale for parents not to show favoritism in raising their children.[24] In retrospect, Yaakov's mistake may seem obvious, and may require further explanation.

---

17. 37:3.
18. See Abravanel.
19. See Sforno 37:3.
20. See Chizkuni 37:3.
21. See Saadia Gaon 37:3; Rashi 37:3; Radak 37:3.
22. The special coat of colors may also indicate that Yosef possessed artistic and creative talents, a characteristic common among children, as well as adults, on the spectrum.
23. 37:4. Abravanel finds it odd that Yaakov gives Yosef a nice garment, which would seem more suitable for a small child than for a young adult as wise as Yosef. See Abravanel 37:1, Question 7. Though Abravanel offers a different understanding of the events, his observation that the garment reflects a childish quality correlates with the interpretation of *na'ar* as indicating childish behaviors on the part of Yosef. If the brothers already disliked Yosef in part because of his immature behaviors, their hatred would be compounded by Yaakov's gift to Yosef, which further accentuated Yosef's childish nature.
24. See Talmud Bavli, Shabbat 10b; *Torah Shelema* [43]; Rambam, Mishneh Torah, Laws of *Nachalot* 6:13. See also Rashbam 37:4; Radak 37:4; Sforno 37:4.

Perhaps Yaakov's actions and errors with respect to Yosef, in this and other episodes, are better understood through a recognition that, as a child exhibiting autistic-like behaviors and characteristics, Yosef is so far from a typical child that Yaakov finds it difficult to navigate the parenting demands that he now encounters. To be sure, Yaakov has faced challenges raising his other children, including conflicts that have arisen among themselves and their mothers, as well as with others.[25] However, despite the need for Yaakov to step in, redirect, and instruct them, if anything, having raised ten relatively typical children, Yaakov is less prepared to be faced with his first child on the spectrum, whose challenges cause conflict in a way that is unfamiliar to him.[26]

---

25. See 30:1–4; 30:14–17; 34:1–31; 35:32.

26. The unprecedented nature of the challenges Yaakov will encounter while navigating Yosef's relationship with his brothers, and the resulting pain he will suffer, may account for the verse that opens these episodes, which states *eyleh toldot Yaakov* ("these are the generations of Yaakov") and then immediately introduces Yosef. 37:2. Although Yaakov has eleven other children, Yosef's special needs occupy so much of his time and attention as a parent that the Torah identifies Yosef and his experiences as the primary embodiment of Yaakov's children.

Indeed, Rashi cites the midrashic statement that Yaakov wished to live in peace, but *rogzo shel Yosef* sprung upon him. Rashi 37:2. After all of the travails that Yaakov has experienced, it is the trials and tribulations surrounding Yosef that will prevent him from finding the peace that he seeks. See *Meleches Machsheves* 37:2; *Chidushei Maran Ri'z haLevi* 37:1. Notably, Rashi's reference to *rogzo shel Yosef* differs from most versions of the midrash, see *Torah Shelema* [9] and note [9], and though presumably denoting "the anger surrounding Yosef," this phrase may also be translated as "the anger of Yosef." Perhaps Rashi is suggesting that Yosef is – or would be justified being – angry at Yaakov, because of his errors, or lack of judgment – or attention – in parenting, resulting from his desire to live in peace.

Such an understanding might also explain why Yaakov is faulted for the seemingly innocuous feeling of wanting to live in peace. Perhaps Yaakov believes that he no longer has to pay close attention to his children, because they are older and because he sees Yosef as so wise. Clearly, however, due to Yosef's behaviors and interactions, this is not the case at all. If so, this understanding likewise draws a connection between the apparent wrongfulness of Yaakov's wish to live peacefully and the manner in which he seems to be punished, through the strife and consternation brought about by the interactions between Yosef and his brothers. Cf. *Chidushei Maran Ri'z haLevi* 37:1.

Accordingly, the lesson the Talmud derives from Yaakov's error may be particularly poignant when directed toward parents or teachers of a child on the spectrum. Adults often design special accommodations for the needs of a child on the spectrum, providing the child additional attention and extra supports. Although these efforts are well-intentioned, and when properly implemented may prove effective, they may also prove futile or even counterproductive when they are not carefully coordinated with the child's peers. If a child on the spectrum is simply singled out for special treatment, rather than enabling the child to integrate into the social environment, a more likely outcome may be jealousy and resentment, resulting in further isolation from other children.[27]

The manner in which the brothers express their hatred of Yosef reflects another dynamic often found in the interactions between children on the spectrum and their peers. Notably, although the text states that as a result of the brothers' hatred, *lo yachlu dabro shalom* ("they could not speak with him peace-

27. Sforno, who sees the garment as a way in which Yaakov demonstrates Yosef's leadership, Sforno 37:3, notes that in spite of their father's command, the brothers refuse to respect Yosef as a leader or even to speak with him in an amicable manner. See Sforno 37:4. Maybe the brothers' hatred of Yosef was triggered less by the garment itself than by the message it represented, which was that Yaakov wished to place Yosef in a position of leadership over them. Yaakov may have attempted to boost Yosef's self-confidence by giving him a position of responsibility, which he thought would likewise improve Yosef's image in the eyes of his brothers. Again, though, well-intentioned efforts by adults to promote the social standing of a child on the spectrum are likely to be unsuccessful, if not counterproductive, if they are not coordinated within the context of the child's social setting.

Moreover, consistent with the views of commentators who interpret the previous verse to indicate Yosef's shepherding skills, Yaakov may have wisely aimed to play off of Yosef's strengths, expecting that the brothers would have no choice but to acknowledge and recognize that Yosef's superior abilities in this area outweigh his social disabilities. Yet, as children on the spectrum sometimes experience, rather than admiring their skills as compensating for social deficits, unsympathetic peers may begrudge and resent their superior skills or strengths as unbefitting someone who is socially inept. Cf. Abravanel (suggesting that the brothers resented Yaakov's additional love for Yosef because in their view, Yosef did not merit special treatment).

ably"),[28] at this point there is no indication that the brothers act in an openly violent or aggressive manner, or even in a verbally abusive way toward Yosef. Instead, the midrash suggests, when Yosef would approach and greet his brothers, they would not answer him.[29] The midrash seems to imply that the brothers' deep-seated hatred prevented them from acknowledging Yosef's presence and his attempts to reach out to them.[30] Because the brothers are "not able" to recognize Yosef as a peer, they simply ignore him, thus engaging in a more subtle – though no less harmful or insulting – form of marginalization.[31]

Another midrash suggests that when Yosef would approach his brothers, they would turn their faces away from him, as if they were unable to respond.[32] It seems somewhat curious, however, that the brothers would engage in such an elaborate charade, rather than expressing their hatred more directly. Moreover, it appears that Yosef does not even notice his brothers' attempts to ostracize him, as he is not deterred from continuing to seek their attention.[33]

Perhaps the brothers have a more pernicious motivation for their actions. Like many children on the spectrum, Yosef may be particularly vulnerable to less open forms of teasing and marginalization, finding it difficult to read the nonverbal cues that are apparent to others. In turn, like many peers of children on the spectrum, the brothers are attuned to Yosef's deficits in perceiving nonverbal messages. Thus, engaging in tactics that do not involve physical or verbal aggression, the brothers carry out a cruel inside joke at Yosef's expense. By ignoring Yosef, or pretending that they do not see him approaching, the brothers succeed in avoiding any communication with him, while at the same time sending a message amongst themselves, affirming both his disability and their intention to continue to marginalize him in the future.

---

28. 37:4.

29. See *Torah Shelema* [56].

30. See also Abravanel.

31. For a more positive interpretation of the brothers' refusal to speak to Yosef, see *HaK'sav V'haKabbala* 37:4.

32. See *Torah Shelema* note [56].

33. 37:5. See Abravanel.

Chapter 3

Yosef's Dreams

> And Yosef dreamt a dream and he told his brothers, and they hated him more. And he said to them, "Listen, please, to this dream that I dreamt. And behold, we were binding bundles in the field, and behold, my bundle rose up and stood, and behold, your bundles gathered around and bowed to my bundle." And his brothers said to him, "Will you be king over us, will you rule over us?" And they hated him more, because of his dreams and because of his words.[1]

The dynamic between Yosef and his brothers deteriorates even further, and more precipitously, as a result of Yosef's dreams and his insistence on telling the substance of his dreams to both his brothers and his father.[2] Clearly, Yosef's dreams are not merely the images he sees when he is asleep. Yosef's dreams represent a fundamental aspect of his character: he is a dreamer, who has dramatic and grandiose visions of himself and his ambitions for the future. Like many children on the spectrum, Yosef is consumed by these visions and unable to place them within the context of his current reality. At this point, he is not a king or leader of a nation, but merely the second youngest of twelve children, with assorted responsibilities toward his father and his brothers – at best, a somewhat precocious, albeit socially awkward, young adult who has strong skills as a shepherd.

Coupled with the immature and unusual social behaviors Yosef has already exhibited, his dreams intensify the brothers'

1. 37:5–8.
2. 37:5–11.

perception of Yosef as an outcast, out of touch with his surroundings and unwilling to recognize the outlandish nature of his visions. Yosef's insistence on telling his dreams to his brothers, in the face of their continuing hatred and their increasingly open derision toward him, typifies the inability of individuals – particularly children – on the spectrum to read social cues and to respond by adjusting their behaviors in a socially appropriate manner.

The first verse in this episode reports that Yosef dreamt a dream and told his brothers, and as an immediate result, the brothers hated him more.[3] As Abravanel notes, the text does not indicate that Yosef has revealed the substance of his dream at this point, yet somehow his actions have intensified his brothers' hatred toward him.[4] According to Chizkuni, Yosef told his brothers what he dreamt, but the text does not record the details because this initial dream did not come to fruition.[5] Another possibility, as Abravanel explains, is that the brothers had a visceral reaction to the mere fact that Yosef continued to seek their attention and companionship after they had distanced themselves from him.[6] Similarly, the mere fact that Yosef tells his brothers that he had a dream may immediately remind them of the qualities they perceive in Yosef and find so annoying, his immaturity and his ambition.[7]

In any event, defying any apparent explanation, Yosef proceeds to tell his brothers the substance of a dream in which he pictures himself ruling over them.[8] By now, Yosef should have gotten the message to stay away from his brothers, not to tell them about his dreams, and certainly not to tell them of

3. 37:5.

4. See Abravanel.

5. Chizkuni 37:5. See also *Meleches Machsheves.*

6. See Abravanel.

7. The brothers' distaste not only for the substance of Yosef's dreams but also for the fact that he was a dreamer and attempted to share his dreams with them may account for the description of their hatred *al chalomotav v'al d'varav* ("because of his dreams and because of his words"). 37:8. The brothers hate both that he has dreams and that he tells them his ambitions. See Ramban 37:8; Abravanel; Sforno 37:8; Malbim 37:5; *HaAmek Davar* 37:5, 8.

8. 37:6–7.

his visions of grandeur in which they will be beholden to him.[9] Moreover, a close reading of the text points to the unusually cheerful and enthusiastic manner in which Yosef approaches and speaks to his brothers, magnifying the seemingly inexplicable nature of Yosef's actions.

According to one midrash, the word *alehem* (to them) is spelled with a *yud* to reflect that Yosef made sure to find an occasion when all of his brothers were gathered together so that he could tell all of them his dream.[10] Likewise, another midrash understands Yosef's introductory phrase, *shim'u na* ("please listen"), as a special pleading to his brothers, indicating that Yosef persists in his efforts even after his brothers refuse his initial attempts to share his dream with them, and even though he knows this will cause them to hate him even more.[11] In a similar vein, Ramban interprets the phrase *shim'u na* as illustrating the joy Yosef feels in telling his brothers his dreams,[12] while Sforno portrays Yosef as insisting that his brothers listen carefully to the dreams and understand their message.[13] Along the same lines, *Meshech Chochma* notes the three times Yosef uses the word *hinei* (behold), emphasizing Yosef's great enthusiasm to share his dreams with his brothers.[14]

In an effort to explain Yosef's puzzling behavior, Abravanel pictures Yosef as so "clean" in his thoughts and so "pure" with respect to his brothers' views of him, that he does not anticipate that telling them his dreams will spark their hatred.[15] Sforno is more critical of Yosef, stating bluntly that Yosef's decision to

---

9. See Abravanel 37:1, Question 11. Apparently unable to fathom how Yosef can fail to recognize the effect these actions will have on his brothers, Radak instead concludes that Yosef wants his dream to upset his brothers, as a form of retribution for their wrongful feelings of jealousy and hatred toward him. See Radak 37:5–7.

10. See *Torah Shelema* [63].

11. See *Torah Shelema* [65], [66], [67].

12. See Ramban 37:8.

13. See Sforno 37:6, 8. See also *Meleches Machsheves; HaAmek Davar* 37:6.

14. See *Meshech Chochma* 37:8.

15. See Abravanel. See also Malbim 37:5 (describing Yosef's "righteousness" and "purity" in believing that his brothers love him); *HaAmek Davar* 37:5.

tell his brothers about his dream is another instance in which Yosef behaves like a childish *na'ar*, failing to take full account of the advisability of his actions.[16] While in some ways these explanations differ considerably, they are both consistent with a portrait of Yosef as having characteristics of a child on the spectrum. Yosef is absorbed in himself and his dreams, seeking the attention of others and trying to bring them into his own world, without acknowledging the realities of the world surrounding him. As impossible as it may be for Yosef's brothers to act with anything but contempt for this dreamer, it is also impossible for Yosef to grasp that his continuing attempts to gain their attention and approval will only marginalize him even further.

Thus, the differing views of Abravanel and Sforno may reflect two sides of the same coin. In some ways, autism spectrum disorder may be associated with a degree of childlike innocence, consistent with Abravanel's explanation that as a result of Yosef's purity, he was oblivious to the negative and hateful feelings of his brothers. At the same time, children of the spectrum can be seen as immature and even foolish in their behaviors, precisely because they fail to appreciate the feelings – often negative – that other children have toward them. In this sense, as a descriptive matter, Sforno seems to state the obvious, that Yosef acted like a childish *na'ar* in his failure to anticipate his brothers' response to his dreams.[17]

Notably, Abravanel is puzzled by the seeming contradiction between Yosef's superior wisdom and his ill-advised decision to tell his antagonists that he envisions them bowing down to him.[18] Yet again, however, for a child on the spectrum, these

16. See Sforno 37:5.

17. As Rav Dessler explains, "It turns out that there is no contradiction at all, for he was called a *na'ar* because of the extent of his holy status; but specifically as a result of this, he was not attuned to matters that are characterized as having the quality of *ma'ase na'arut*, i.e., a lack of thought and consideration regarding the external nature of the matters, that is to say, how they will appear in the eyes of others.... We understand that through his deficits [*chesrono*], the Torah reveals the extent of Yosef's exalted status...." See *Michtav M'Eliyahu* 2:229.

18. 37:7. See Abravanel 37:1, Question 11.

different characteristics are not contradictory, but rather different manifestations of the same condition. A child on the spectrum may possess, at once, both advanced cognitive skills and severe social deficits. The ability to engage in higher intellectual thinking is not inconsistent with – and in some cases may correlate directly with – an inability to understand the feelings of others and engage in socially appropriate behaviors.

The enthusiasm that *midrashim* and commentators identify in Yosef's decision to tell his brothers his dreams is likewise consistent with autism spectrum disorder. Yosef's childlike impulsivity, coupled with the excitement he feels about his dreams and his self-absorbed ambitions, compels him to share his visions with others – unaware of the obvious and immediate effects on his brothers, and unable to pause and contemplate the eventual danger to himself. Children on the spectrum are often so captured by their own interests and desires that they act on them impetuously, oblivious to the feelings or perceptions of others. Like Yosef, once they have begun to engage their own passions and interests, in word or in action, individuals on the spectrum may not know when to stop, or may be unable to bring themselves to do so.

When the brothers react to his first dream with expected hatred,[19] Yosef is not deterred from dreaming another dream and again, inexplicably, sharing the contents of the dream with them.[20] Significantly, the brothers register their displeasure with Yosef's first dream through the use of rhetorical questions, asking sarcastically: "Will you be king over us, will you rule over us?"[21] It is common for individuals on the spectrum to face challenges in understanding nonverbal messages, such as sarcasm, conveyed through facial expressions and tone of voice that may accompany and imply an additional meaning beyond the literal meaning of the spoken words. Perhaps Yosef misunderstood the brothers' mocking response as an affirmative statement, professing their acceptance of the validity of his dream and their belief that one day his dream will come to frui-

19. 37:8.
20. 37:9.
21. 37:8.

tion.[22] If so, it is not surprising that Yosef would feel vindicated and empowered to keep dreaming.

> And he dreamt another dream and he told it to his brothers, and he said, "Behold, I dreamt another dream, and behold, the sun, the moon, and eleven stars were bowing to me." And he told his father and his brothers, and his father rebuked him and said to him, "What is this dream that you dreamt? Are we going to come, I and your mother and your brothers, to bow to the ground before you?" And his brothers were jealous of him, and his father observed the matter.[23]

Yosef's insistence on telling his brothers about his second dream seems to illustrate even further his stubborn and self-absorbed visions and ambitions.[24] While the first dream pictured the brothers' bundles bowing down to Yosef's,[25] the second dream has the sun, the moon, and eleven stars – apparently alluding directly to Yosef's father, mother, and brothers – bowing down to Yosef himself.[26] This time, Yosef tells his dream to his father as well, predictably prompting his brothers' further resentment, but also provoking a negative reaction from Yaakov.[27]

---

22. Although Yaakov's negative response to Yosef's second dream is likewise framed as a sarcastic question, "Are we going to come, I and your mother and your brothers, to bow to the ground before you?" 37:10, Yaakov's reference to Yosef's deceased mother demonstrates even to Yosef that Yaakov finds the dream impossible and incredible. See Rashi 37:10; Radak 37:10. In addition, the text introduces Yaakov's words with the term *va'yig'ar bo* ("and he rebuked him"), 37:10, possibly indicating that the mocking nature of Yaakov's words was clear even to Yosef, while the brothers' words are introduced with the neutral term *va'yomru* ("and they said"), 37:8, possibly implying that the negative meaning of their words was more subtle and therefore escaped Yosef's grasp.

23. 37:9–11.

24. See Ramban 37:10; Sforno 37:10; Abravanel 37:20 (commenting on the phrase "Let us see what becomes of his dreams.")

25. 37:7.

26. 37:9.

27. 37:10. According to Abravanel, Yosef expected that telling his second dream to his brothers in his father's presence would demonstrate Yosef's love for his brothers, and elicit their love and respect for him. Once again, however, as Abravanel notes, Yosef's actions toward others bring

Although Yaakov loves Yosef, at this point he has become exasperated by Yosef's interactions with his brothers, and he finds it necessary to respond. Maybe Yaakov realizes that the favoritism he has shown toward Yosef, aimed at defusing the conflicts between Yosef and his brothers, has only increased the brothers' hatred of Yosef. Yaakov's mocking response to Yosef's dream – "Are we going to come, I and your mother and your brothers, to bow to the ground before you?"[28] – might be an attempt to mollify the brothers,[29] demonstrating that Yaakov is capable of chiding Yosef as well. In reprimanding Yosef, Yaakov expressly rejects, among other aspects of the dream, the implication that the brothers will bow down before Yosef.

Taken together, Yaakov's efforts to navigate the parenting challenges posed by Yosef and his brothers are typical of attitudes and strategies parents or teachers sometimes employ in attempting to resolve tensions between children on the spectrum and their peers. Yaakov first tries to accommodate Yosef with extra attention, giving him a colorful coat as a sign of leadership or to suit his personality, only to find that this treatment marginalizes Yosef even further from his brothers, and that Yosef seems to have viewed his father's extra attention as a confirmation of his own self-centered visions.

When Yaakov sees that Yosef has dreams of grandeur that are literally delusional in their scope, as they include Yosef's deceased mother,[30] Yaakov can only react with outrage and frustration.[31] As Ramban, Abravanel, and Sforno note, Yaakov recognizes that dreams reflect a person's hopes and thoughts, and he faults Yosef for having such outlandish ambitions.[32] Moreover, according to Ramban, Yaakov is upset by the childish nature of Yosef's dreams and visions,[33] which Yaakov may find difficult to reconcile with his picture of Yosef as a young

---

about precisely the opposite result of what he intends and anticipates.

28. 37:10.

29. See Rashi 37:10; Ramban 37:10; Chizkuni 37:10; Abravanel.

30. See Talmud Bavli, Berachot 55a–b; Rashi 37:10; Radak 37:10; Abravanel.

31. 37:10.

32. See Ramban 37:10; Abravanel; Sforno 37:10.

33. See Ramban 37:10.

man possessing the wisdom of an adult. However, children on the spectrum are prone to have an exaggerated self-image and unrealistic aspirations, and again, cognitive abilities do not prevent childish dreams and behaviors. It would appear, then, that Yaakov continues to have trouble understanding and appreciating Yosef's condition, which would account for the qualities Yaakov finds so exasperating.

Whatever the motivation behind Yaakov's caustic reaction to Yosef's dream, the brothers respond with jealousy.[34] While their negative response is to be expected, it may be surprising that the brothers feel jealous only now, after Yosef recounts his second dream both to them and to Yaakov.[35] According to many commentators, the brothers now have a reason to envy Yosef, either because his willingness to tell his dream to Yaakov is a reflection of their father's esteem for Yosef,[36] or because the substance of the second dream convinces them of Yosef's elevated status.[37] Yet, the chronology of the text suggests that the brothers' jealousy arises not when Yosef recounts the dream, but only after Yaakov admonishes Yosef.[38] If anything, however, as commentators observe, Yaakov's remarks were intended to defuse the brothers' hatred and to alleviate any jealousy they felt toward Yosef.[39]

Perhaps the dynamic between Yosef, his brothers, and their father can be better understood in light of another common characteristic among children on the spectrum, a tendency to engage in attention-seeking behaviors. When the child receives attention – including, somewhat paradoxically, negative attention – the reaction from others serves to reinforce the child's inclination to repeat those behaviors. This understanding may help explain Yosef's insistence on telling his brothers his

34. 37:11.

35. 37:11.

36. See Sforno 37:11.

37. See Abravanel; *HaK'sav V'haKabbala* 37:9; Malbim 37:11; *HaAmek Davar* 37:11; *Beis Halevi* 37:9.

38. 37:10–11. Cf. *Torah Shelema* [90] (connecting the brothers' jealousy with Yaakov's reaction); *Meleches Machsheves* 37:11.

39. See Rashi 37:10; Ramban 37:10; Chizkuni 37:10; Abravanel.

dreams – not in *spite* of their hatred, but as part of an effort seeking their attention.[40]

At the start of the story, Yaakov showers Yosef with love and positive attention,[41] sparking the brothers' hatred.[42] When the brothers refuse to speak to Yosef,[43] he tells them his first dream, possibly with the objective – conscious or otherwise – of provoking their negative attention.[44] The brothers subsequently break their silence, expressing their hatred through a harshly worded response,[45] which may, in turn, provide Yosef the impetus to tell them his second dream.[46]

Significantly, however, when Yosef recounts his second dream to them, his brothers do not react.[47] At this point, they may have become attuned to Yosef's pattern of behavior, which they refuse to reinforce. Rather than engaging Yosef in another argument, they simply do not give him the attention they realize he has been seeking.[48]

Sensing his inability to elicit any response from his brothers, Yosef recounts his second dream to Yaakov.[49] Perhaps unaware of the factors motivating Yosef's impulsive behavior, Yaakov reacts in a way that is designed to deter Yosef, but instead provides him the negative attention he was unable to generate in

---

40. 37:4–8.

41. In addition to the textual descriptions of the attention Yaakov showed Yosef – when he listened to Yosef's negative reports about his brothers, 37:2, and when he gave Yosef the woolen coat that expressed his love for Yosef over the brothers, 37:3 – according to Ramban, Yaakov selected Yosef as his companion, who did not leave his side. See Ramban 37:3 (interpreting the description of Yosef as *ben zekunim* to Yaakov).

42. 37:3–5.

43. 37:4. See *Torah Shelema* [56] and note [56]; Abravanel; *HaK'sav V'haKabbala* 37:4.

44. 37:5–8. Cf. Radak 37:5–7 (explaining that Yosef told his brothers his dream because he wanted to upset them). See also Abravanel.

45. 37:8.

46. 37:8–9.

47. 37:9. See Abravanel; *HaAmek Davar* 37:9.

48. Indeed, according to Netziv, Yosef did not request that his brothers listen to his second dream because he knew they were not interested. See *HaAmek Davar* 37:9. As such, he may have instead been trying to annoy and provoke them.

49. 37:10. Cf. *Meleches Machsheves* 37:10.

his brothers. The brothers now become jealous of Yosef – not because of the substance of the second dream, but because they are envious that Yosef continues to be the focus of Yaakov's attention, whether positive or negative.

As the episode concludes, Yaakov sees what is happening, but he does not actively intervene.[50] Perhaps Yaakov is carefully observing the interactions between Yosef and his brothers, with the aim of eventually trying to find a way to resolve their disputes.[51] On a basic level, Yaakov may be watching carefully over the situation, to make sure the brothers do not harm Yosef out of their feelings of hatred and jealousy. If so, as is often the case with children on the spectrum and their peers, Yaakov is able to deter Yosef's brothers only when he asserts his direct supervision as an authority figure. Once Yosef is left unsupervised, he will no longer be protected from harm.

50. 37:11.

51. See *Meleches Machsheves* 37:11. A midrash states that Yaakov took a quill and wrote down the day, the time, and the place of the events. See *Torah Shelema* [92]. In contemporary terms, maybe Yaakov is taking data of the different incidents, to compile a record of Yosef's interactions with his brothers and put together a plan of behavior for them.

Chapter 4

Yaakov Sends Yosef to His Brothers

> And Yisrael said to Yosef, "Are your brothers not shepherding in Shechem? Go and I will send you to them." And he said to him, "Here I am." And he said to him, "Go, now, see to the welfare of your brothers and the welfare of the sheep, and bring back to me a report . . . ."[1]

Yaakov's inability to manage the conflict between Yosef and his brothers is even more evident in the episode that immediately follows. Having witnessed the brothers' animosity toward Yosef, Yaakov nevertheless enthusiastically[2] sends Yosef on a mission to find them in Shechem.[3] Yaakov's motivation so defies explanation, that many commentators can only characterize his actions as serving an inadvertent role in facilitating God's plan to ultimately lead the nation to Egypt, in accordance with the promise to Avraham (Abraham).[4] While this perspective is undoubtedly correct as a depiction of God's dominion over the course of history, on a human level, Yaakov seems oddly oblivious to the danger his instructions will bring to Yosef,[5] placing

1. 37:13–14.
2. See Abravanel.
3. 37:13–14.
4. See Talmud Bavli, Sotah 11a; *Torah Shelema* note [107]; Rashi 37:14; Radak 37:13; Ramban 37:14–15. See also *Mei Hashiloach* 37:1.
5. Abravanel similarly emphasizes that, although the brothers' treatment of Yosef undoubtedly serves to further God's ultimate plan, they remain responsible for the wrongfulness of their actions, which were the product of their own free will. See Abravanel 37:34.

him alone with his brothers, far from the protective watch of their father.[6]

It may be possible that Yaakov simply does not understand the nature, degree, or underlying causes of the hatred the brothers feel toward Yosef. Yaakov has had his own concerns about Yosef, but his interactions with Yosef are different. Though he feels some measure of frustration with Yosef's actions and attitudes, as an adult and as his father, Yaakov is willing to overlook and compensate for many of the behaviors that are so annoying and infuriating to Yosef's siblings.

To be sure, Yaakov is no stranger to sibling rivalry and hatred, having been the target of Esav's (Esau) threats and recriminations.[7] However, the bitter and open animosity that repeatedly arose between Yaakov and Esav, which included Esav's explicit desire to harm Yaakov,[8] differed fundamentally from the more subtle kinds of marginalization Yosef experiences at the hands of his brothers. It may not prove surprising that Yaakov is unable to detect manifestations of this less common and, to him, unfamiliar form of hatred.

Adults who are quick to identify and react to open expressions of physical bullying and abuse among children often fail to recognize or appreciate less blatant – but no less hurtful or harmful – instances of verbal or even nonverbal bullying and ostracism, which often confront children who have social deficits. Accordingly, despite having observed some of the tension and taunting his sons directed toward Yosef in the past, Yaakov does not envision the brothers posing a physical danger in the future.[9]

---

6. See *Torah Shelema* [95], [108]; Rashi 37:14; Radak 37:13; Rashbam 37:13; Chizkuni 37:13; Ramban 37:14; Abravanel.

7. See 27:36, 41–45; 32:4–33:16.

8. See 27:41–45.

9. See Radak 37:13 (Yaakov did not think the brothers would harm Yosef; had Yaakov suspected them, he would not have sent Yosef); Abravanel (Yaakov was not worried that the brothers would harm Yosef because "he knew that Yosef had never harmed them, so why would they hurt him?").

However, Abravanel suggests, the brothers initially set out for Shechem both for the purpose of getting away from Yosef and with the thought that, should Yosef follow them, they would have an opportunity to take out their anger against him. Apparently, Yaakov was unable to detect or

Moreover, Yaakov finds it particularly difficult to fathom that his own son – and his favorite son, who is so wise – would not be able to navigate the hatred of others. After all, Yaakov had been confronted with the threats and machinations of two of the most scurrilous and dangerous characters in the Torah, Lavan (Laban) and Esav, and he had survived and prevailed by outmaneuvering both of them.[10] Yaakov can only expect that Yosef, who has displayed wisdom well beyond his years, will likewise find a way to withstand the comparatively minor slights and indignities he faces from his brothers. Again, though, like many children on the spectrum, Yosef cannot rely on his advanced cognitive abilities to protect himself from the very real peril engendered by his social deficiencies, largely invisible to adults but fully apparent to his peers.

Alternatively, maybe Yaakov has begun to recognize some of Yosef's social deficits, and the decision to send Yosef to find his brothers represents an attempt by Yaakov to find a way to include Yosef in an activity with his peers. When the brothers set off with their sheep, Yosef is left alone with Yaakov, highlighting his isolation from his brothers. Yaakov may look at the situation as an opportunity for Yosef to interact with his brothers in a positive and productive manner.[11] Indeed, when attempting to integrate children on the spectrum in activities with their peers, it is often helpful to provide clear and simple directions for a discrete and direct form of social interaction.

Thus, Yaakov instructs Yosef simply to find his brothers, to inquire about them and the sheep, and to report back to him. Yaakov may be hoping that this brief interaction between Yosef

---

anticipate their scheme.

10. See 27:18–29; 30:31–43; 31:20–32:1; 32:4–33:16.

11. Abravanel suggests that Yaakov enthusiastically encouraged Yosef to rejoin his brothers, rather than remain at home with Yaakov, which would further marginalize Yosef from the other sons. Sensing the brothers' resentment that Yosef has been set apart as special, Yaakov now wants Yosef to participate in the same activity with them.

According to Sforno, Yaakov specifically sends Yosef on a mission in which he will be expected to demonstrate and exercise his wisdom, by observing his brothers and, if necessary, correcting any errors he finds. See Sforno 37:14.

and his brothers, which they will all understand to be at the behest of their father, will enable the brothers to relate to Yosef in a different setting, and potentially to see him in a different light. Commentators note that Yaakov's instruction for Yosef to find out about the *shalom* (welfare) of the sheep[12] seems a bit unusual,[13] but given Yosef's demonstrated skill as a shepherd, Yaakov may have seen this mission as an opportunity for Yosef to feel more comfortable and more confident, and to display his talents to his brothers.[14]

Still, despite the best of intentions and the ostensible logic underlying Yaakov's plans, his failure to fully appreciate the form and degree of Yosef's social disabilities leads Yaakov to have unrealistic hopes and expectations. As adults sometimes fail to realize, for children on the spectrum, even the most seemingly simple social interactions may be fraught with peril. Outside of Yaakov's protective watch, Yosef is left vulnerable to his brothers' devious schemes.[15]

Yosef's enthusiastic response to Yaakov's request[16] seems even more inexplicable, given the repeated hatred Yosef's brothers expressed directly toward him. While the brothers may have succeeded, at times, in eluding Yaakov's notice, Yosef would presumably have been well aware of the full extent of their feelings. In reality, however, children on the spectrum are often unaware of the way their peers view them, and of the impact their own words and behaviors have on the way they are treated. Moreover, children with autism spectrum disorder

12. 37:14.

13. See *Torah Shelema* [103] and note [103]. Moreover, there does not appear to be a compelling reason for Yaakov to send a messenger for this information, see Chizkuni 37:14, let alone Yosef, see Sforno 37:14; *HaAmek Davar* 37:13; *Torah Temima* 37:2, note 9, thus suggesting that Yaakov had an additional goal and motivation in sending Yosef.

14. See Sforno 37:14.

15. See Ramban 37:14 (noting that the brothers were able harm Yosef because they were far from their father); Abravanel (suggesting that the brothers went far away in part so that they might have more of an opportunity to harm Yosef).

16. The response *hineni* ("here I am") signifies Yosef's ready acceptance of Yaakov's mission. See 37:13; Rashi 37:13; Abravanel.

sometimes place an unduly high degree of trust in the wisdom, judgment, and power of adults and authority figures.

Thus, Yosef dutifully follows the instructions of Yaakov, with abiding faith that his father knows best and has the ability to insure his safety.[17] The midrash states that later, Yaakov would look back at this episode with regret and painful incredulity, asking why Yosef was so willing to go seek out his brothers even though he knew they hated him.[18] The answer, which likely would have seemed similarly incomprehensible to Yaakov, may be that Yosef was unable to process and understand his broth-

---

17. See Radak 37:13 (Yosef believed his brothers would not harm him because of their fear of their father).

Ohr Hachaim suggests that Yaakov used the phrases "I will send you . . . and bring back to me," 37:13–14, to imply that, in case Yosef was worried about his brothers' hatred, he would be protected as a *shaliach mitzvah* (an agent for a good deed) who is fulfilling his father's request. Of course, Yosef was ultimately harmed as a result of following his father's instructions, leading *Ohr Hachaim* to offer a complex analysis of why the general principle, that a *shaliach mitzvah* will not face harm, was not operative in this case. See *Ohr Hachaim* 37:13–14.

Alternatively, Yaakov's statement "I will send you to them," 37:13, may be intended to provide Yosef a measure of reassurance, giving him the confidence that, although Yaakov will not accompany him, Yosef will be able to rely on the authority of his father to ward off any of his brothers' attempts to harm him. Though tragic, it need not be surprising that, contrary to the expectations of both Yaakov and Yosef, assertions of Yaakov's distant authority will be insufficient to protect Yosef from his brothers.

Although adults are sometimes under the impression that they can simply instruct a child on the spectrum to "tell your friends that I sent you," absent the direct supervision of the authority figure, the child's peers – especially those who have already engaged in bullying – are unlikely to be deterred from committing further acts of abuse. If anything, instructing a child with social deficits to assert the authority of an adult figure may lead to further resentment on the part of the child's peers, particularly in a situation like Yosef's, in which his brothers already detest him for the special relationship he has with their father.

Moreover, because children on the spectrum sometimes have an overabundance of trust and respect for authority figures, and because they are often unable to understand the feelings of others, they may assume their peers will exercise the same level of obedience to the directions of teachers, parents, and other adults. As a result, Yosef was blissfully unaware of the dangers he would face in following Yaakov's instructions and advice.

18. See *Torah Shelema* [97].

ers' hatred or the danger it posed to his physical and emotional safety and security.[19]

> . . . And he arrived at Shechem. And a man found him and behold he was wandering in the field, and the man asked him, "What are you seeking?" And he said, "I am seeking my brothers, please tell me where they are shepherding." And the man said, "They have traveled away from here, because I heard them saying, 'Let us go toward Dotan [Dothan].'" And Yosef went after his brothers and he found them in Dotan.[20]

When Yosef arrives at Shechem, his journey is interrupted by yet another unusual episode, a meeting with an unnamed man who finds Yosef wandering in the field.[21] It may not be surprising that Yosef is lost,[22] given that children on the spectrum often have spatial and other sensory deficits, coupled with a degree of self-absorption leading them to be somewhat oblivious to their physical surroundings, all of which impact their sense of direction.[23]

By observing Yosef, the man can apparently see that he is

---

19. According to one version of the midrash, Yaakov regretted that, though he himself knew of the brothers' hatred, he still sent Yosef to them. See *Torah Shelema* [97]. According to another version, Yaakov regretted that Yosef accepted the mission so eagerly, even though Yosef knew the brothers hated him. See *Torah Shelema* note [97]. Some *rishonim* likewise held the view that Yosef was aware of his brothers' animosity toward him. See, e.g., Rashi 37:13; Radak 37:13; Rashbam 37:15.

20. 37:14–17.

21. 37:15.

22. According to Ramban, Yosef had wandered off the path and did not know where to go. See Ramban 37:15. Radak writes that after he reached Shechem and did not find his brothers, Yosef "was going here and there" to try to find them and was wandering in the field. See Radak 37:15. Similarly, Sforno writes that Yosef was "going here and there" to try to find his brothers. See Sforno 37:15.

23. Yaakov may have sensed Yosef's deficits in this regard as well. Perhaps for this reason, the text seems to indicate that Yaakov escorts Yosef some distance, from the city of Hebron to the Valley of Hebron, before sending him off to Shechem. See 37:14; *Torah Shelema* [106] and note [106]; Radak 37:14; Chizkuni 37:14; Sforno 37:14. Abravanel writes that Yaakov escorted him because he loved Yosef.

lost, and so he asks what Yosef is seeking.[24] Without any further introduction, Yosef replies that he is looking for his brothers, and he requests that the man tell him where they are.[25] Strikingly, Yosef assumes that upon a momentary encounter, a total stranger will have the ability to identify him, associate him with his brothers, and provide him information about his brothers' whereabouts. Commentators note the unusual nature of Yosef's assumptions,[26] apparently prompting Radak and Ibn Ezra to insert into Yosef's request the additional words: "if you know."[27] Though understandably hopeful, Yosef should at least acknowledge the distinct possibility that this man – whoever he may be – will not be able to respond helpfully, for any number of reasons.

In reality, however, individuals on the spectrum, who are absorbed in their own interests and concerns, sometimes hold the belief that others, including strangers, will be absorbed in their world as well. They may further incorporate these beliefs into the way they relate to and interact with others, leading them to behave in a manner that will be perceived as unusual or difficult to understand. According to the text, Yosef does not add any qualifiers to his request to this man, or otherwise show any indication that he considers the perspective of the person he has just met. Instead, he carries on the conversation only from his own perspective, with the assumption and expectation that a stranger is familiar with him and his family, and will know where he can find his brothers.

Yosef's reaction to the man's response is likewise both unusual and telling. When the man informs Yosef that the broth-

24. 37:15.

25. 37:16.

26. See, e.g., *Ohr Hachaim* 37:16; *HaAmek Davar* 37:15.

27. See Radak 37:16; Ibn Ezra 37:16. Apparently prompted both by the unusual nature of Yosef's request and by the man's knowledgeable response, a number of *midrashim* and commentators conclude that this man is, in fact, an angel, which could account for Yosef's expectation and anticipation that he would be privy to this information. See, e.g., *Torah Shelema* [109], [110], [111], [112], [120], [122]; Rashi 37:15; Ramban 37:15, 17; *HaAmek Davar* 37:15. However, Ibn Ezra emphasizes that, on a *p'shat* level, the man was simply a human passerby. See Ibn Ezra 37:15.

ers have gone away and that he heard them saying they would go to Dotan,[28] Yosef has an opportunity to reflect on his relationship with his brothers, and possibly to assess the dangers he might face if he continues to pursue them. Following the lead of several *midrashim*,[29] a number of commentators suggest that the man's use of the phrase *nas'oo mi'zeh* ("they have moved away from here") contains an implicit warning to Yosef that his brothers have moved away from their fraternal relationship with him, and they are now planning to harm him.[30] Nevertheless, without any note of caution or hesitation, Yosef persists in his single-minded determination to fulfill his father's instructions, immediately making the fateful decision to travel to Dotan and find his brothers.[31]

Yosef's inability or unwillingness to heed the man's warning seems to reflect, at once, both an element of recklessness and an admirable allegiance to the wishes of his father. Indeed, Ramban praises Yosef for the devotion he showed to his father in the face of various forms of adversity that could easily have deterred him from completing his mission.[32] At the same time, though, Ramban is puzzled that Yosef would place himself in danger after being told that his brothers were plotting against him.[33] Ramban suggests that the phrase *nas'oo mi'zeh* did not provide Yosef an explicit warning of his brothers' intention, but rather, it carried a dual-meaning: the literal meaning, that the brothers had physically departed from that place, and the deeper, secondary meaning, that they had figuratively departed from their brotherly feelings toward him.[34] Because Yosef did not understand the deeper meaning, Ramban explains, he instead proceeded in accordance with the literal meaning, and continued to pursue his brothers in Dotan.[35]

However, Ramban's explanation begs the further question,

---

28. 37:17.
29. See *Torah Shelema* [117], [118], [119], [121], and note [117].
30. See Rashi 37:17; Ramban 37:17; Abravanel; *Ohr Hachaim* 37:17.
31. 37:17.
32. See Ramban 37:15.
33. See Ramban 37:17.
34. See Ramban 37:17.
35. See Ramban 37:17. See also *Ohr Hachaim* 37:17.

left unaddressed, as to why Yosef was unable to understand the meaning hidden in the man's message.[36] This question becomes even more difficult in light of Ramban's earlier interpretation of *ben zekunim* as connoting Yosef's advanced wisdom,[37] which presumably should have equipped him to comprehend the man's words on a deeper and more advanced level.[38] As with many of the apparent mysteries and seeming contradictions latent within both Yosef's remarkable journey and the varied and complex portraits of his personality and his interactions with others, a plausible answer may be found in contemporary insights into strengths and challenges that often coexist in the lives of individuals on the autism spectrum.

Individuals on the spectrum often have an overly structured and stubbornly inflexible view of the world around them and their role within it. Their resulting refusal to adapt to change may present as a form of arrogance or obstinacy, but it may, in fact, stem from internal insecurity growing out of the need to navigate and find a sense of order and purpose amidst otherwise confusing and confounding surroundings. From their perspective, it is quite understandable that once a sense of order is achieved, it will be carefully guarded and not easily surrendered. Having been provided a structured path to follow, an individual on the spectrum will sometimes make every effort

36. See *Ohr Hachaim* 37:17; *HaAmek Davar* 37:17. Echoing the approach of various commentators in response to seemingly inexplicable events that occur, and puzzling actions that are taken, at various points of the story of Yosef, Netziv finds this question so confounding that he concludes that Yosef's inability to understand the secondary meaning of the man's statement was by Divine decree, for the purpose of bringing about the ensuing events. See *HaAmek Davar* 37:17. *Ohr Hachaim* suggests that Yosef believed this man was human, not an angel, and therefore understood the man's words on a human level, without contemplating their deeper meaning, which was based in the man's angelic status. See *Ohr Hachaim* 37:17.

37. See Ramban 37:3.

38. Perhaps it is due to the strength of this question that Rashi, after citing the midrashic interpretation of the figurative meaning behind the man's statement, seems to step back from this interpretation, adding the uncommon and, in this context, otherwise somewhat anomalous and unusually placed reminder that *eyn mikra yotze midei peshuto* ("a verse cannot go outside of its plain meaning"). See Rashi 37:17; Mizrachi 37:17.

and, if necessary, exert enormous inner strength and fortitude, to adhere to that path until reaching its conclusion.

Yosef's previous experiences typify an individual struggling to find his place in the world, where he can fulfill his dreams and establish meaningful relationships with his peers. To his complete surprise and continuing confusion, his sincere efforts to express himself and share his ideas, though aimed at developing a connection with others, have instead earned him nothing but the hatred of his brothers and even the scorn of his father who loves him. Against this backdrop, Yaakov's instructions offer Yosef a carefully structured setting, within which lies the opportunity for him to fulfill a clearly defined role in the close environs of his immediate family; sure enough, Yosef jumps at the opportunity.

Yet, Yosef soon finds himself, once again, utterly lost and alone, literally and metaphorically wandering in the field. Seeking to regain the structure he so desperately craves, Yosef persists in trying to follow through on his father's command. When he meets a man who appears to have the information that will allow him to return to his prescribed role, Yosef jumps at this opportunity as well, without so much as contemplating the possibility that the man's ostensibly helpful words carry a hidden note of caution. Yosef's failure to understand the hidden message may result, in part, from his refusal to consider any message beyond the one he wants to hear.

Of course, as Ramban emphasizes, Yosef's exercise in perseverance exemplifies his fidelity to Yaakov.[39] Though he may seek structure, Yosef insists on finding that structure not in mundane pursuits, but specifically for the purpose of fulfilling the wishes of his father. In the face of numerous obstacles and available excuses, Yosef refuses to submit to the challenges he confronts, or to consider failure as an available option. Thus, Yosef turns a potential weakness into the very source of the great strength he will require to continue the journey to his brothers. Whatever the origins of his stubborn persistence – including, perhaps, a form of disability – Yosef transforms his internal limitations and emerges with the determined ability,

39. See Ramban 37:15. See also Rashbam 37:15.

against very long odds, to honor his father and carry out his instructions.

Ramban's depiction of Yosef as unable to grasp the figurative meaning of the man's statement is consistent with another characteristic common among individuals on the spectrum, the inability to read nonverbal cues. Individuals with autism spectrum disorder often have an overly literal perception of words and actions they observe, in part because they are absorbed in their own perspective of the world, leading them to disregard the actual aims and intents of others. The result may be a failure to recognize secondary messages the speaker is intending to convey, through body language, tone of voice, inflection, or other additional forms of communication.

Perhaps, then, Yosef's inability to understand the man's implicit warning stems from Yosef's tendency, which he has exhibited in the past[40] and may again exhibit in the future,[41] to perceive the words and actions directed at him entirely through the prism of his own experiences and views of the world, ascribing to them his own limited and literal perspective. Moreover, as Yosef continuously demonstrates, his world is characterized by an allegiance to the truth, as he sees it, preventing him from acknowledging subtlety or ambiguity in the words or actions of others. Although this man is a total stranger, Yosef immediately accords to him the trustworthiness due to an authority figure, which implies to Yosef a similar allegiance to straightforward truth. In short, Ramban may see within Yosef the possibility for both advanced intellectual acuity and limited social awareness.

In contrast to Ramban's approach, Abravanel maintains that given Yosef's great wisdom, there is no doubt he is able to recognize the hints of caution contained in the man's words.[42] According to Abravanel, however, Yosef consciously disregards the warning, determined to follow his father's command, and confident that God is steering him along his destined path.[43] Notably, Abravanel's explanation may also be consistent with a

40. See 37:8.
41. See 41:38.
42. See Abravanel.
43. See Abravanel.

portrait of an individual on the autism spectrum. In Abravanel's depiction, Yosef ignores the realities of the world around him, refusing to heed the clear warning signs before him – not because he is oblivious to the danger, but out of a stubborn and inflexible pursuit of fulfilling his assigned task, and a self-assured sense of fulfilling his own destiny.

In this view, notwithstanding both his wisdom and an awareness of his surroundings, Yosef nevertheless exhibits another kind of innocence, a naiveté of sorts, believing that his trust in his father, in God, and in himself will protect him from the clear danger that looms in front of him. A similar quality of innocent self-assuredness sometimes characterizes individuals on the spectrum, who are unwilling or unable to conform their behavior to the more realistic expectations of society.

At the same time, whatever the source of Yosef's determination, like Ramban, Abravanel praises Yosef for his resolute adherence to his father's instructions. Once again, differing approaches to understanding Yosef may reflect different sides of the same coin, each capturing different aspects of the complexity of autism spectrum disorder.

When Yosef arrives in Dotan, the narrative quickly shifts, focusing on his brothers and the way they treat and regard him. At this point in the episode, Yosef, who has been the central character and whose actions have moved the course of the story, now plays a passive role. Yet, by implication, a close look at the brothers tells much about Yosef as well. The cruel insensitivity the brothers display toward Yosef provides a revealing portrait of the kinds of attitudes, passions, and actions children on the spectrum often – albeit innocently and unwittingly – bring out in their peers.

Before Yosef can even approach his brothers, they see him from a distance and plot to kill him,[44] tellingly referring to Yosef not by his name, but by the title *ba'al hachalomot* (dreamer).[45] They continue to hate him because he is a dreamer, literally and, quite likely, figuratively as well. Indeed, after formulating their plan, the brothers mockingly retort, "Let us see what becomes

44. 37:18.
45. 37:19.

of his dreams,"[46] demonstrating their continued resentment of the ambitious visions he has shared with them.[47]

The nature of the different strategies the brothers devise and the sentiments they express, throughout the process of attempting to avoid and ultimately rid themselves of Yosef, may symbolize and correspond to methods of marginalization and invalidation that are sometimes used as a way of dealing with the unpleasant or inconvenient presence and behaviors of individuals on the spectrum. At the outset, the brothers' decision to venture out toward Shechem was, according to Abravanel, intended as part of an effort to distance themselves from Yosef, who they expected would remain at home with Yaakov.[48] When they see Yosef approaching, the brothers realize that they have failed in their attempt to keep away from him, but they cannot imagine that they will have to tolerate him. Thus, the brothers immediately embark upon a plan to kill Yosef and throw him in a pit,[49] a solution that, though remarkably brutal, apparently seems necessary to them as a means of removing this irritant from their midst. All the while, Yosef's brothers marginalize and dehumanize him amongst themselves, using the derisive label *ba'al hachalomot*[50] and ridiculing his outlandish ambitions,[51] thereby desensitizing themselves to the cruel nature of their own scheme.[52]

---

46. 37:20. Ramban notes the mocking nature this phrase. See Ramban 37:20. Likewise, perhaps the brothers' initial exclamation *hinei*, introducing their declaration that the *ba'al hachalomot* is approaching, 37:19, is intended to mock Yosef's repeated use of the exclamation *hinei* when he excitedly insisted on telling them about his dream. See *Meshech Chochma* 37:8. Their mocking then turns quickly into determined hatred, signified by the transitional word *v'ata* (and now), 37:20, indicating their resolve to take immediate action. See Radak 37:20.

47. According to Abravanel, this statement reflects the brothers' suspicion that Yosef's descriptions of the dreams were themselves stories that Yosef invented, not his actual dreams. See Abravanel. See also *HaK'sav V'haKabbala* 37:19; *HaAmek Davar* 37:8.

48. See Abravanel.

49. 37:18–20.

50. 37:19.

51. See Ramban 37:20.

52. Likewise, the brothers may have thereby desensitized themselves to any of Yosef's screams for mercy while they were carrying out their

The pattern of the brothers' reactions toward Yosef mirrors, albeit in extreme fashion, attempts by those who, as a result of their own intolerance or insecurity, go to great lengths to avoid individuals with autism spectrum disorder. Like Yosef's brothers, they may initially proceed from a general degree of dislike or discomfort, to a more personal form of resentment for having to interact with peers or others who are on the spectrum. They may then begin to experience strong feelings of frustration, exacerbated by the unfamiliar and annoying behaviors they are witnessing, culminating in violent outbursts aimed at eliminating the person they view as the source of their frustration. In an effort to ease their consciences and deflect their own responsibility, they may resort to various forms of marginalization and dehumanization, including mocking and belittling the victim of their aggression.

Significantly, Sforno suggests that the brothers may have validated their scheme to kill Yosef through their belief that Yosef was planning to find fault in them or instigate them, in a way that would imperil their standing in the eyes of Yaakov or God.[53] Of course, Yosef had no such plan. Instead, the brothers' rationalization seems to resemble attitudes and assumptions, common among both peers and adults, that the unusual behaviors of a child on the spectrum are intentional or, somehow, even malicious, thus justifying and inviting cruel and insensitive responses. In many of these instances, the all-too-common refrain, typical of the temptation to blame the victim, tends to be along the lines of "they asked for it." In reality, though, similar to the reactions of Yosef's brothers, these attitudes and assumptions are simply – and tragically – at best, erroneous and misguided projections of those who are intolerant and insecure, and at times, unconvincing justifications for truly inexcusable conduct.

For his part, Yosef remains seemingly and strangely oblivious to his brothers' intentions.[54] Perhaps he is so focused on

---

scheme. See 42:21; *Torah Shelema* 37:24 note [142]; *Torah Shelema* 42:21 [78].

53. See Sforno 37:18.

54. As Malbim comments on the phrase "Yosef walked after his

completing his mission for Yaakov that, like many children on the spectrum, he fails to take into account the nuance and complexity of the situation, inflexible to change and rigidly resistant to reconsidering his course of action. Moreover, Yosef is likely unable to read his brothers' body language, preventing him from having even a clue as to the nature of their plans.[55] In the eyes of his brothers who see him walking toward them, Yosef may now appear to be in an odd, nearly dreamlike state, reminding them of the behaviors that had initially elicited their hatred toward him.[56] In fact, *midrashim* suggest that when Yosef later reaches his brothers,[57] he displays a sense of joy or praise,[58] apparently presenting a form of self-satisfaction or outward appreciation for finding them.[59] Accordingly, Yosef continues on his way, falling directly into their trap.[60]

---

brothers," he continued to consider them as brothers. See Malbim 37:17. See also *Ohr Hachaim* 37:16.

55. According to *HaK'sav V'haKabbala*, the brothers declared their plan to kill Yosef loudly enough for him to hear, though their true intent was only to scare him. See *HaK'sav V'haKabbala* 37:18, 19, 20. In any event, Yosef continued to approach them, undeterred by their words or their actions.

56. Indeed, *midrashim* use the reflexive verb *mitga'eh* (proud of himself) to describe Yosef's self-absorbed joy as he now approaches his brothers, see *Torah Shelema* note [139], evoking similar midrashic descriptions of the immature and self-stimulatory behaviors that characterized Yosef as a *na'ar* and initially triggered his brothers' animosity. See *Torah Shelema* [33] and note [33].

57. 37:23.

58. See *Torah Shelema* [139] and note [139].

59. See *Torah Shelema* note [139].

60. 37:17, 37:23. A midrash questions Yosef's apparent silence during the time that he is later sold. See *Torah Shelema* 42:21[78]. Although the midrash concludes, based on the brothers' later remarks, see 42:21, that Yosef begged each of them for mercy, see *Torah Shelema* 42:21 [78], the entire episode seems to depict Yosef as detached and oblivious to the reality of events around him and the nature of the brothers' hatred toward him.

According to another midrash, Yosef called from inside the pit, asking – at length but to no avail – what he has done that has caused them to place him in the pit. When the brothers hear his screaming and crying, rather than showing any degree of pity, they move away so they will not hear him anymore. See *Torah Shelema* 37:24 note [142]. This midrash captures both

When Reuven (Reuben) hears his brothers' plan, he counsels them not to kill Yosef but instead to throw him into a pit.[61] Although Reuven intends to eventually save Yosef and bring him back to Yaakov,[62] the brothers seem to take his suggestion as an alternative – and possibly somewhat less violent – method of eliminating Yosef. When Yosef finally reaches them, the brothers immediately – and with apparent haste[63] – tear off his coat, throw him into the pit, and begin to sit down to eat.[64]

A number of commentators observe the repetitive identification of Yosef's coat in this verse, not merely as *kutanto* (his coat), but also as *ketonet hapassim* (the fine woolen coat).[65] As some explain, the brothers specifically target the coat, which Yaakov gave to Yosef, as the source of their jealousy and hatred toward their brother.[66] Along these lines, the brothers may likewise be trying to repudiate Yaakov's efforts to demonstrate Yosef's special talents. Like many children on the spectrum whose peers are unable or unwilling to acknowledge the strengths that adults sometimes recognize, bereft of this symbol of his potential leadership and success, Yosef is treated as nothing more than an uncouth and irritating pest. The brothers may now feel justified throwing him into the pit, which serves their purposes of both isolating him and putting him out of their mind, as they promptly sit down and eat a meal.[67]

---

the extent of the brothers' cruel disregard for Yosef and, concomitantly, Yosef's utter inability to understand the depth of their hatred for him, or even to realize what has prompted their animosity toward him.

61. 37:21–22.

62. 37:22.

63. See Maharam 37:23.

64. 37:23–25.

65. 37:23.

66. See Rashi 37:23; Radak 37:23; Chizkuni 37:23. But see Rashbam 37:23, who offers a different explanation.

67. See Abravanel (noting the degree of cruelty this represents on their part). In contemporary terms, the brothers' method of socially isolating Yosef by eating a meal without him evokes a situation common in school settings, where children on the spectrum are often excluded by their peers and left to eat lunch on their own. Indeed, during later episodes, Yosef is again depicted, in the text and in the midrash, as separated from his brothers while eating his meal. See 43:32; *Torah Shelema* 50:15 [49] and note [49]; Rashi 50:15. Although in the later instances it is Yosef's choice

Ultimately, when the brothers see a caravan of merchants pass by, Yehudah (Judah) convinces the others that, rather than killing Yosef – rather than harming their brother with their own hands and covering up what they have done – they should instead sell him.[68] While arguably less disturbing than the plan to kill him, the decision to sell Yosef is, of course, far from innocuous, and in other ways reflects the peculiar nature of the brothers' hatred toward Yosef. For example, the midrash and a number of commentators note that the price of the sale, twenty silver pieces,[69] seems quite low.[70] Abravanel explains that the brothers were willing to accept a relatively small sum for Yosef, because their primary goal was not to profit monetarily, but to distance him from themselves and their father.[71] Sforno adds that the notion of selling Yosef as a slave appealed to the brothers as a fitting response to his ambitious dreams of leadership over them.[72] Similarly, other commentators cite the midrashic statement, that the brothers used the proceeds of the sale to purchase shoes, as a further indication of their intention to degrade and devalue Yosef.[73]

Thus, the brothers embrace the opportunity to sell Yosef as a particularly effective avenue of expressing their hatred and jealousy of his dreams, his personality, and his behaviors. Yosef will be taken to another land, leaving the brothers free from any interaction with him, and free to disclaim responsibility for any harm that may befall him. To their relief, like many on the spectrum whose peers, family, and other caretakers are too overwhelmed or too uncaring to continue, Yosef is now someone else's concern, and someone else's problem. Toward this end, beyond their callous disregard for Yosef, when they return to Yaakov the brothers are willing to betray and deceive

---

to eat on his own, these scenarios may similarly highlight his continued social isolation.

68. 37:25–27.

69. 37:28.

70. See *Torah Shelema* [167]; Chizkuni 37:28; Abravanel (citing Rashi); Commentary to Sforno 37:27 (Mossad Harav Kook).

71. See Abravanel.

72. See Sforno 37:27.

73. See *Torah Shelema* [167] and note [167].

their father, to inflict great pain upon him, and to ignore and exacerbate his ongoing suffering.[74]

Meanwhile, notwithstanding the brothers' somewhat dubious claim that they found a bloody coat, and their abrupt demand that Yaakov identify whether the coat was his son's,[75] Yaakov immediately concludes that Yosef was eaten by a wild animal,[76] absolving the brothers of any blame or suspicion. Apparently puzzled by Yaakov's reaction, commentators insert additional facts into the narrative, suggesting, for example: that the brothers sent the coat by messenger, to avoid facing Yaakov's possible accusations;[77] that the brothers brought the coat before Yaakov and manufactured a story to avoid his suspicions;[78] or that Yaakov's remark that Yosef has been torn up should be understood as a question, as to how it was possible that Yosef was eaten by an animal with no remains to be found.[79]

Whatever means the brothers employed to mislead their father, it remains striking that Yaakov, who has previously demonstrated such aplomb in dealing with the deception of others, is utterly unaware that his sons are the true source of his pain. Once again, the most simple – and most plausible – explanation may be that, with all of his experience, wisdom, cleverness, and mental dexterity, because he is an adult, Yaakov is still unable to fathom the nature and depth of the hatred children can have toward their peers who are on the spectrum, the dangers they pose, and the harm they are willing to inflict.

At the close of this episode, Yaakov is seen in deep mourning for Yosef, and despite the efforts of all of his children, he refuses to be comforted.[80] Although Rashi cites the midrash[81] suggesting that Yaakov could not be consoled because Yosef was still alive, other commentators offer explanations more consistent with Yaakov's apparent belief that Yosef had died. According to

74. 37:32–34.
75. 37:32.
76. 37:33.
77. See Ramban 37:32; Chizkuni 37:32.
78. See Ramban 37:32.
79. See Abravanel.
80. 37:33–36.
81. See *Torah Shelema* [202]; Rashi 37:35.

Radak and Chizkuni, Yaakov mourns so deeply and is unwilling to accept the consolation offered by his family because he blames himself for placing Yosef in danger by sending him off alone.[82]

Perhaps upon reflection, Yaakov has begun to recognize Yosef's deficits, and he feels responsible for not putting sufficient protections in place against the peril that appears to have befallen his son. Of course, though Yosef was harmed while attempting to fulfill his father's instructions, the source of harm was, in fact, not an animal, but Yosef's brothers. Notably, then, although in reality Yaakov bore some responsibility for what occurred to Yosef, Yaakov's own feelings of guilt are somewhat mistaken and misplaced.[83]

Yaakov's difficulties in this regard may reflect yet another aspect of the challenges facing parents of children on the spectrum. Up until this point, despite his best intentions, Yaakov seems to have been largely unaware of the unique obstacles Yosef faces and, as a result, unsuccessful in protecting his son. Even in retrospect, upon realizing that he should not have sent Yosef on his own, Yaakov fails to learn the real lesson of these events, believing instead that Yosef was the victim of a wild animal.

Parents of children on the spectrum often have particular difficulty recognizing and evaluating the nature and likelihood of the dangers confronting their children, failing to identify which of these threats they can ameliorate or mitigate and which are beyond their control. As a result, tragically, they may deny or remain unaware of their own responsibility for consequences they could have prevented, and instead accept responsibility for outcomes that were simply not their fault.

82. See Radak 37:34; Chizkuni 37:35.

83. Although Sforno writes that Yaakov blames himself for sending Yosef "to his brothers," see Sforno 37:35, given that at this point Yaakov appears to believe that Yosef was killed by a wild animal, Sforno's approach would seem to similarly suggest that Yaakov generally regrets sending Yosef away without protection, but not that he suspects that Yosef's brothers harmed him.

Chapter 5

Yosef in the House of Potiphar

WHEN WE NEXT ENCOUNTER Yosef, he is in Egypt, in the house of Potiphar, the *Sar HaTabachim* (Chief Slaughterer).[1] We are told that Yosef is successful because God is with him, which is apparent to Potiphar, who then appoints Yosef to be in charge of his house and all that he has.[2] Yosef's immediate and immense success in this new setting stands in sharp contrast to the travails and indignities he suffered at the hands of his brothers.[3]

Yet, the text does not identify the manner or methods behind Yosef's success, other than to repeat that God's blessings accompanied him.[4] Evidently, notwithstanding his sudden change of fortunes at the hand of God, Yosef himself has not changed, as there are no indications that he engages in any socially appropriate dialogue or interactions. In fact, it appears that Yosef still has the same qualities and characteristics that infected his relationship with his brothers, and his inability to anticipate and navigate social challenges will again lead him into trouble.

---

1. 39:1.
2. 39:2–4.
3. Abravanel notes the appearance of the word *va'yehi* (and it was) three times in the verse introducing Yosef's success. 39:2. Abravanel suggests that each of the three phrases beginning with the word *va'yehi* reflects a separate aspect of the mercy God granted to Yosef in bringing about his success. In a similar vein, these phrases may highlight the degree to which Yosef's sudden and substantial success contrasts with the constant, tragic, and nearly fatal failure he experienced in his previous setting with his family.
4. 39:5.

> . . . And Yosef was handsome in form and of nice appearance. And it was after these events, his master's wife lifted her eyes toward Yosef, and she said, "Lie with me." And he refused . . . And it was, when she propositioned him every day, and he did not listen to her . . . And it was, on that day, he came to the house to do his work, and no man of the house was there in the house. And she grabbed him by his garment, saying, "Lie with me." And he left his garment in her hand and fled and went outside.[5]

The Torah describes Yosef as *yefei to'ar* (handsome in form) and *yefei mar'eh* (of nice appearance),[6] prompting the attentions of Potiphar's wife.[7] Commenting on the description of Yosef as *yefei to'ar,* and paraphrasing a midrash, Rashi states that when Yosef sees he is successful, he begins to eat and drink and to twirl his hair.[8] In this reading of the midrash, Rashi continues, God rebukes Yosef for playing with his hair while his father, Yaakov, is mourning over him, leading God to "send the bear" toward Yosef in the form of Potiphar's seductive wife.[9] Again, however, a close look at alternate versions of the midrash quoted by Rashi provides grounds for a different way of understanding both Yosef's behaviors and the way others react to him.

First, unlike Rashi, who offers his comments to explain the verse describing Yosef as *yefei to'ar,* several *midrashim* cite Yosef's behaviors in the context of expounding upon the following verse, which tells us that "after these events, his master's wife lifted her eyes toward Yosef."[10] As supercommentators on Rashi note, the text implies that Potiphar's wife was drawn to Yosef not merely because of his intrinsic good looks, docu-

5. 39:6–8, 10–12.

6. 39:6.

7. 39:7.

8. See Rashi 39:6; *Torah Shelema* [44], [53]. See also *Torah Shelema* [103] (citing *Zohar Chadash* on 39:12, describing Yosef as fixing his clothes and twirling his hair, thereby provoking Potiphar's wife to grab him by his garment and proposition him).

9. See Rashi 39:6.

10. See 39:7; *Torah Shelema* [44], [53], and notes [44], [53].

mented in the previous verse, but because of an occurrence she observed that caught her attention – namely, Yosef's conduct.[11]

Second, in the process of listing Yosef's behaviors, rather than including eating and drinking alongside twirling his hair, an alternate version of the midrash describes Yosef as tending to his eyes and lifting his heels.[12] Strikingly, these are the same behaviors identified in midrashic illustrations of the earlier description of Yosef as a *na'ar* (child).[13] Apparently, Yosef is now reverting to some of the same impulsive and self-stimulatory behaviors that marked him to his brothers as a *na'ar* – an immature dreamer, a child on the spectrum, whom they found deserving of and susceptible to their marginalization, hatred, and, ultimately, physical violence.

If so, the connection between Yosef's conduct and Potiphar's wife's overtures might be seen in a different light. When Potiphar's wife looks at Yosef, she not only observes that he is a handsome young man. She also notices that he is engaged in childish, self-absorbed, and dreamlike activities, signaling his inability to effectively navigate his surroundings, and his vulnerability to the attacks – or, in her case, the advances – of others, particularly adults in positions of authority. His behaviors label him as a child on the spectrum, innocent and naïve, rendering him attractive to her as a convenient target for her predatory appetites.

In further contrast to Rashi's explanation, which seems to criticize Yosef for enjoying himself while his father mourns, thereby incurring God's punishment, this version of the midrash depicts Yosef as self-confidently declaring his own strength and success, prompting God to "send the bear" to confront Yosef.[14] Thus, the midrash draws a more direct connection between Yosef's actions and Potiphar's wife's response. Without

11. See, e.g., *Divrei Dovid* 39:6 (cited in Chavel's edition of Rashi) (the word *va'yehi* in place of *haya* implies that something occurred to bring about or accentuate Yosef's good looks); Mizrachi 39:6 (the phrase *achar had'varim ha'eyleh* ("after these events"), 39:7, implies that something transpired that caused her to notice him).

12. See *Torah Shelema* [44].

13. See *Torah Shelema* 37:2 [33].

14. See *Torah Shelema* [44].

referencing Yaakov, whose mourning seems tangential, at best, to Yosef's current situation, this midrash instead faults Yosef for conduct that is self-centered and self-satisfied.[15] Perhaps Yosef's precipitous success has gone to his head, leaving him complacent in the belief that his dreams are beginning to come to fruition. Potiphar's wife, in turn, uses this opportunity to take advantage of Yosef, as his brothers did earlier, by recognizing and exploiting his obvious obliviousness to the dangers that surround him. In some ways, in this reading, the misfortunes Yosef now encounters seem more a natural consequence of his self-absorbed behavior than Divine retribution for any wrongdoing on his part.

When Potiphar's wife first propositions him, Yosef refuses her advances.[16] Yosef's courageous resistance against the pressure she exerts, captured in the word *va'yema'eyn* ("and he resisted"), is dramatically emphasized through the cantillation of an extended *shalshelet*.[17] On one level, Yosef's determination to withstand her demands is a powerful act of defiance against

---

15. This understanding of Yosef's conduct and subsequent misfortune may be more consistent with another version of the midrash, which quotes Yosef as thanking God, at this time, for allowing him to forget his father's house. See *Torah Shelema* note [53]. Rather than faulting Yosef merely for enjoying himself while his father mourns, this midrash depicts Yosef as engaging in self-centered pursuits for the express purpose of distancing himself from his past experiences in Yaakov's house. In turn, this same self-absorption leaves Yosef vulnerable to Potiphar's wife's machinations.

In yet another version of the midrash, God chides Yosef for being *mitga'eh b'atzmecha* ("proud of yourself") while Yaakov mourns. See *Torah Shelema* note [53]. The term *mitga'eh,* which the midrash likewise uses to describe Yosef as he approaches his brothers in Dotan, see *Torah Shelema* 37:23 note [139], evokes the similarly reflexive verb *mitga'ga* that the midrash uses to portray Yosef as a *na'ar*. See *Torah Shelema* 37:2 note [33]. In all three cases, the midrash paints a picture of Yosef as being focused on himself rather than appreciating the feelings of others. This conduct is not only dangerous to Yosef, rendering him oblivious to threats he faces; in connection with Yaakov, Yosef's insensitivity and lack of regard for the feelings of his father are arguably blameworthy and deserving of punishment.

16. 39:7–9.

17. See 39:8; *Torah Shelema* [56] and note [56]; *HaK'sav V'haKabbala* 39:8.

his master's forceful wife.[18] More significantly, Yosef's ability to exercise self-control is particularly notable in light of the impulsivity that he has repeatedly exhibited in the past.

Yosef now appears to be showing distinct signs of maturity and growth in areas that, thus far, have proved to be challenging and detrimental to him. Yosef accompanies his rejection of Potiphar's wife with an eloquent speech adamantly proclaiming his fidelity to his master and his commitment to his own sense of morality.[19] In contrast to the nearly fatal mistakes he made in his awkward conversations with his brothers and his father, Yosef now speaks convincingly and successfully, with wisdom, confidence, and authority. Moreover, when Potiphar's wife persists in her demands, Yosef seems to enlist, to his own advantage, his stubborn sense of self-regard, enabling him to muster the strength to brazenly reject her daily entreaties.[20]

Notwithstanding these indications of progress, however, Yosef remains a *na'ar*, unable to fully read Potiphar's wife's intentions and to anticipate and navigate her manipulations and maneuverings. In the course of his otherwise impressive speech to her, Yosef goes too far, invoking not only his loyalty to Potiphar but his fidelity to God as well.[21] While the reference to Potiphar might resonate with his wife, it seems unlikely that she will be persuaded by Yosef's insistence that he not sin against God. If anything, mentioning his God will only serve as a reminder to Potiphar's wife that Yosef is an *Ivri* (Hebrew), and indeed, she will later exploit his outsider status as part of her effort to incriminate him.[22] Nevertheless, exhibiting another common characteristic of children on the spectrum, Yosef speaks to Potiphar's wife with the same zeal and enthusiasm he used in telling his brothers of his dreams. He is unable to stop

18. As Rabbenu Bachya notes, the verse specifically describes her as "his master's wife," emphasizing Yosef's courage in defying her. See Rabbenu Bachya 39:8.

19. 39:8–9.

20. See 39:10; Rabbi Yosef Dov Soloveitchik, *Divrei Hashkafa* 201. See also Rabbi Hershel Schachter, *B'Ikvei Hatzoan* 2.

21. 39:9.

22. See 39:14.

himself from speaking the truth, as he sees it, even if it will later be used against him.

Similarly, despite Yosef's success in fending off Potiphar's wife's daily advances, his inability to fully understand the modus operandi underlying her scheme impedes him from looking at the big picture and anticipating the more dangerous threats that he will soon confront. Like a child on the spectrum, Yosef perceives his situation only from his own self-absorbed perspective, leaving himself in a position of having to react anew to each of her attempts, rather than recognizing her pattern of behavior and preventing it from recurring.

Having missed all the warning signs, Yosef continues to arrive at Potiphar's house to do his work, until one day he finds himself alone in the house with Potiphar's wife.[23] As Chizkuni notes, the text introduces this event with the phrase *va'yehi k'hayom* ("and it was on that day"), implying that to Yosef, this was a day just like any other day.[24] As the midrash suggests, however, this was not just another day for Potiphar's wife, who engineered the situation by selecting an occasion when she

23. 39:11. At least one commentator observes how unusual it would seem for Yosef to be oblivious to the dangers of entering Potiphar's wife's room when they are alone in the house. See *HaK'sav V'haKabbala* 39:11. Noting the verse's emphasis that Yosef entered the house "to do his work," 39:11, *HaK'sav V'haKabbala* explains that Yosef felt compelled to complete his work, as ordered by his master, and thus he was forced to enter the room of his master's wife, notwithstanding the peril that would await him. See *HaK'sav V'haKabbala* 39:11.

This explanation is consistent with the actions of a child on the spectrum, whose condition brings about a need for structure, a rigid compliance with the directions of an authority figure, and a stubborn insistence on completing a task, manifested by an inability to be flexible even when necessary and appropriate in response to new and unexpected circumstances. Indeed, the same unrelenting adherence to Yaakov's instructions had likewise compelled Yosef to continue to seek out his brothers even in the face of warning signs that he should have recognized, but that he refused or was unable to see. Conversely, Yosef ultimately escapes the encounter with Potiphar's wife through a similarly stubborn adherence to what he understands to be the instructions of his father, not to give in to her temptations and demands. See Talmud Bavli, Sotah 36b.

24. See Chizkuni 39:11.

knew nobody else would be present.[25] As such, Yosef walks right into her trap, blissfully unaware;[26] he is no match for her cunning and manipulative calculations and machinations.

On that fateful day, Yosef is abruptly confronted by Potiphar's wife, whose verbal demands are now coupled with physical coercion, yet he continues to maintain his morality, suddenly and silently refusing her entreaties, escaping from her grip, and fleeing outside.[27] Yosef has once again prevailed, overcoming his impulsive behavior in a way that earns him the title *Yosef Hatzadik* (Yosef the Righteous). While his moral strength would be commendable for anyone in his situation, for Yosef, the ability to withstand both his characteristic impulsivity and his self-indulgent behaviors merits the badge of righteousness.

The midrash states that Yosef's source of strength is a vision of his father Yaakov, cautioning Yosef that if he sins with Potiphar's wife, his name will be erased from amongst those of his brothers on the *choshen* (breastplate of the High Priest).[28] Notably, Yosef exhibited a similar single-minded determination to follow his father's instructions to accompany his brothers, in the face of obstacles that would have provided convenient excuses for him to avoid the task he had been given.[29] Though his previous efforts to join his brothers had ultimately proven detrimental to Yosef, in the process of attempting to complete his mission, he developed and demonstrated important qualities of loyalty to his father and to his own sense of morality. Now, faced with the nearly insurmountable challenges posed by Potiphar's wife, Yosef again places his trust in his father's

25. See *Torah Shelema* [91], [92]; Rashi 39:11; Chizkuni 39:11.

26. Sforno suggests that Yosef entered a room within the building, unaware that Potiphar's wife was already present in the room. See Sforno 39:11.

27. 39:12.

28. See Talmud Bavli, Sotah 36b; *Torah Shelema* [100] and note [100]; Rashi 39:11. Although most versions of the midrash depict Yosef as seeing an image of Yaakov in a *chalon* (window), at least one version states that Yosef saw Yaakov's image in a *chalom* (dream). See *Torah Shelema* note [100]. In this reading, Yosef may be relying on one of his unique talents, his ability to see the truth through dreams, as a means toward finding the strength to overcome his behavioral challenges.

29. See Ramban 37:15

authority and refuses to surrender to temptations and excuses that were likely available to him. Here too, according to the midrash, Yosef follows his father's admonitions for the purpose of securing his place among his brothers, a goal that had eluded him since his earliest interactions with them. This time, Yosef's allegiance to his father works to his own benefit – at least momentarily.

Despite this temporary triumph, however, Yosef loses the larger battle, as his stubborn strength is no match for Potiphar's wife's ability to quickly size up the situation and cleverly manipulate her social surroundings. Without pause, she calls out to the members of her house and begins to manufacture a narrative that depicts the facts in a way that absolves her of any fault and places the blame squarely on Yosef.[30] Keenly aware of the perceptions and biases of her listeners, she identifies Yosef as an *ish Ivri* (a Hebrew man).[31] For the Egyptians, particularly those associated with the noble house of Potiphar, labeling Yosef as a loathsome *Ivri*[32] immediately stigmatizes him as an outsider who is not to be trusted. At the same time, she is careful to refer to Yosef as an *ish* rather than a *na'ar*,[33] dispelling any possible notion that she has taken unfair advantage of the vulnerable and unsuspecting individual that she knows Yosef to be.

Having rehearsed her version of the events, and having apparently succeeded in convincing her household of the veracity of her account – however implausible – Potiphar's wife is now ready to convince her more important audience, her husband, as well. Using some of the same coded language to disparage Yosef, she refers to him as *ha'eved ha'Ivri* (the Hebrew servant) and accuses him of attacking her.[34] Again displaying her devious ability to place herself in the mindset of her listeners,

30. See 39:14–15; Sforno 39:12, 14.

31. 39:14.

32. See Ramban 39:14; Abravanel. See also Rashbam 43:32; Ramban 41:38.

33. Her use of the word *ish* (man) appears to be an intentional characterization of Yosef as a mature adult, in contrast to the use of the word *na'ar* (child) by the *Sar HaMashkim* (Wine Butler), to describe Yosef years later. 41:12.

34. 39:17.

Potiphar's wife crafts her remarks in a way that leaves her husband in the position where he must take her side over that of the lowly *Ivri* servant. Though it appears somewhat likely that Potiphar does not fully believe her story, if at all,[35] he is left with no other choice but to send Yosef to prison.[36] She has used her advanced social skills and emotional intelligence to outsmart Yosef, whose moral strength and determination, along with his actual innocence, are woefully insufficient in the face of her manipulative exploitation.[37]

---

35. See *Torah Shelema* note [118]; Ibn Ezra 39:19; Sforno 39:19; Ramban 39:19 (citing a midrash); Abravanel. See also Chizkuni 39:20 (citing a midrash); *Meshech Chochma* 39:20 (citing Targum Yonasan).

36. See Abravanel; Sforno 39:19.

37. A close reading of Potiphar's wife's speeches may help uncover the full extent of her shameless and self-serving artifice. See Nechama Leibowitz, *Studies in Bereishis* (Hebrew) 294–97.

> And she called to the men of her house and she spoke to them, saying, "Look, he has brought to us a Hebrew man to play with us" . . . And she said to [Potiphar] like these words, saying [*kad'varim ha'eyleh laymor*], "He came to me, the Hebrew servant that you brought to us, to play with me " . . . And it was, when his master heard his wife's words, that she told him, saying, "Like these things, your servant did to me [*laymor kad'varim ha'eyleh asa li avdecha*]" and he grew angry. 39:14, 17, 19.

When she calls to the members of her house, Potiphar's wife implicitly places the blame on her husband, declaring, "Look, he has brought to us an *ish Ivri l'tzachek banu*" ("a Hebrew man to play with us"). 39:14. Although it would be unseemly for her to refer to Potiphar by name in this context, see Ramban 39:14, the message is clear. She has successfully established that Potiphar is at fault for what has allegedly occurred, setting the stage to put him on the defensive when she confronts him directly with her version of the events.

When Potiphar returns home, she is again slyly ambiguous in the way she recounts what has occurred, telling her husband, *ba elay ha'eved ha'Ivri asher heveta lanu l'tzachek bi* ("he came to me, the Hebrew servant that you brought to us, to play with me"). 39:17. Rashi inverts the order of these words, instead rendering the verse to read: *ba elay l'tzachek bi ha'eved ha'Ivri asher heveta lanu* ("he came to me to play with me, the Hebrew servant that you brought to us"). See Rashi 39:17. Supercommentators suggest that Rashi finds this inversion necessary because the linear reading of the verse implies that Potiphar's wife is accusing him of bringing Yosef to them for the purpose of having an affair with her. See Mizrachi 39:17; *Gur Aryeh* 39:17.

Alternatively, though, Potiphar's wife might cleverly be going further on the offensive, avoiding any culpability for her own infidelity by implicitly deflecting the blame not only onto Yosef, but onto her husband, who is, after all, responsible for bringing Yosef to their house. Her underhanded phraseology has the advantage of being susceptible to more than one interpretation, thereby allowing her to feign a naive innocence while at the same time directly placing Potiphar on the defensive by hurling an unstated accusation at him. See also Sforno 39:19.

Viewing Potiphar's wife in this light might also offer an alternate understanding of the broader sequence and wording of the narrative in this episode, particularly the repeated use of the cryptic phrase *kad'varim ha'eyleh*. The text introduces Potiphar's wife's statement to him with the phrase: "And she said to him *kad'varim ha'eyleh laymor*," followed by "*ba elay ha'eved. . . .*" 39:17. The text then states that: "[Potiphar] heard his wife's words, that she told him, *laymor kad'varim ha'eyleh asa li avdecha*, and he grew angry." 39:19. Rashi cites the midrashic interpretation of the second use of the phrase *kad'varim ha'eyleh*, in verse 19, as a reference to an act of intimacy. However, other commentators question the plausibility of this interpretation on a number of grounds. See, e.g., Ramban 39:19. Moreover, both Rashi's explanation and other interpretations seem to ascribe a different meaning to each of the two uses of a single phrase in very close proximity. Although it is certainly possible that the same phrase has different meanings depending on the specific context, it may be preferable to find a common meaning in both cases.

Perhaps the phrase *kad'varim ha'eyleh* is used in both verses as an indication of the essential message of the words, in one case to the speaker and in the other case to the listener. In the first case, in speaking these words, the important message that Potiphar's wife is trying to convey is that she is innocent and that Yosef and Potiphar are to blame. The verse emphasizes that she accomplishes this by using "words like these": *ba elay ha'eved . . .*, 39:17, i.e., coded and subtle language that absolves herself of any wrongdoing while casting aspersions on both Yosef and Potiphar. In the other case, turning to what Potiphar hears her saying, the verse emphasizes the important message to him, captured in the essence of "words like these": *asa li avdecha*. 39:19. Although many aspects of his wife's statement would presumably have been troubling to Potiphar, hearing that "your servant did [this] to me" was the element of her accusations that most angered him, as these three words – *asa li avdecha* – captured her ability to place the blame squarely on him and on Yosef.

This reading may also be consistent with Radak's comments on the phrase *kad'varim ha'eyleh* in verse 17. Radak interprets the use of the comparative conjunction "like" to imply that these were not the precise words spoken, but that they were "more or less" the words used, which conveyed their essential meaning. See Radak 39:17. See also *Ohr Hachaim* 44:7. Applying Radak's understanding, in the context of verse 19 as well, might suggest that the verse is likewise conveying the essential meaning of

Children on the spectrum are vulnerable to the false accusations of others, who are all too often willing and able to take advantage of an unpopular and socially inept outsider. In particular, both peers and adults may use a child on the spectrum as a scapegoat, who will be blamed for their own misdeeds – including, in an exceptionally cruel twist, their own victimization of that child. Likewise, Yosef is unable to muster any response to Potiphar's wife's carefully contrived false accusations, through which she escapes her own culpability by shifting the blame onto the true victim. Instead, he is forced to remain silent and accept the painful and unfair reality of his undeserved punishment in prison.

the words used, this time as heard by Potiphar.

Chapter 6

Yosef in Prison

WHEN PLACED IN PRISON, Yosef finds favor in the eyes of the *Sar Beit HaSohar* (Warden of the Prison), who appoints him to a position of leadership over the other prisoners.[1] Once again, the text attributes Yosef's sudden and substantial success entirely to God's graces, without describing any specific words, actions, or skills on Yosef's part that might have played a role in helping him achieve his success.[2] In this setting, however, Yosef will soon have an opportunity to demonstrate some of his unique talents and, for the first time, to begin to utilize his advanced cognitive abilities in a way that will benefit – and impress – others around him. Still, as is common for both children and adults on the spectrum, in the course of displaying his undeniable – and seemingly unbelievable – gifts, Yosef will also comport himself in a way that accentuates his continuing social challenges, preventing him from reaping the benefits of his brilliant insights.

Some time after Yosef is placed in prison, he is assigned to the *Sar HaMashkim* (Wine Butler) and the *Sar HaOphim* (Chief Baker), who have been imprisoned for their transgressions toward the King of Egypt.[3] One morning, after they have each dreamt what they apparently believe to be a significant dream, Yosef approaches them.[4] When Yosef looks at them, he

1. 39:20–22.
2. 39:21–23.
3. 40:1–4.
4. 40:5–6.

observes that they appear unsettled, and he asks them, "Why are your faces disturbed today?"[5]

On one level, Yosef seems to show considerable social progress, recognizing the feelings of others and initiating a conversation through a thoughtful inquiry as to the cause of their feelings. Yosef appears to have moved beyond his earlier status as a *na'ar*, who acted in a childish, shortsighted, foolish, and self-centered manner. Instead, Yosef has emerged as a socially aware and empathetic individual, whose interactions with others are not only socially appropriate but reflect a wisdom that the midrash associates with other important biblical figures.[6] It may be particularly notable that Yosef perceives the feelings of the *Sar HaMashkim* and the *Sar HaOphim* based on their facial expressions, before they have spoken to him. Unlike his previous encounters, when Yosef seemed to miss nonverbal cues that likely would have helped him understand the speakers' intentions,[7] he now reads and understands the feelings others convey in their nonverbal expressions, without the need for them to speak any words.

Alternatively, though, Yosef may once again be displaying characteristics sometimes found among individuals on the spectrum. Along with – and perhaps as a cause of – their challenges reading nonverbal cues during conversations, individuals with autism spectrum disorders often fail to make eye-contact when speaking with others. It has been suggested that the reluctance to look others in the eye is not a symptom of an inability to read into their faces, but a result of an ability to see too much in facial expressions. Under this theory, individuals on the spectrum may stare too intently when conversing with others, making them self-conscious of their own pronounced focus on another person's face, and in turn causing them to look away. If so, Yosef's ability to read the expressions of the *Sar HaMashkim* and the *Sar HaOphim*, specifically without any accompanying conversation, may be consistent with, rather than an exception

5. 40:6–7.
6. See *Torah Shelema* 40:7 [17].
7. See 37:8; 37:17.

to, autistic-like behaviors.[8] Indeed, typifying the experiences of many individuals on the spectrum, Yosef continues to interact with the *Sar HaMashkim* and the *Sar HaOphim* in ways that reflect, at once, both strengths and weaknesses, demonstrating the special wisdom and talents he possesses while also causing further obstacles to be placed in his path toward reaching his true potential.[9]

---

8. Along these lines, the social deficits that prevent individuals on the spectrum from reading nonverbal cues may, at times, be limited to messages that others intend to communicate with them. Somewhat paradoxically – though likewise consistent with social ineptitude – individuals on the spectrum are sometimes adept at reading body language or tone of voice to uncover messages the speaker wishes to conceal from them. Accordingly, notwithstanding his repeated obliviousness to seemingly obvious – but unstated – messages that were directed toward him, Yosef has the ability to decipher, from the expressions on their faces, the unstated feelings that the *Sar HaMashkim* and the *Sar HaOphim* do not plan to share with him.

As yet another alternative, it may be significant that Yosef's apparent progress in recognizing the feelings of others occurs specifically in the context of their reactions to their dreams. Yosef's ability to read social cues may be limited to situations in which he is demonstrating his ability to read dreams, providing him the self-confidence to interact in a socially effective manner.

9. Further along these lines, Ramban observes, rather than simply stating that Yosef "asked them" why they appeared troubled, the verse depicts Yosef as asking "the noble servants of Pharaoh who were with him in the prison of the house of his master." 40:7. According to Ramban, this detailed description highlights the courage Yosef displays: a lowly slave and *na'ar*, detested by his master, approaches the King's noble servants, who can have him killed at their will, asks them the source of their disquiet, and offers interpretations of their dreams. Moreover, Ramban adds, Yosef demonstrates brave confidence in his own wisdom when he interprets the dream of the *Sar HaOphim* to be a harbinger of doom. After all, if Yosef's interpretation proves to be wrong and the *Sar HaOphim* survives, he will likely have Yosef killed. See Ramban 40:7. Cf. *Meshech Chochma* 40:2.

Yet, once again, as is common among individuals on the spectrum, characteristics that arguably demonstrate Yosef's virtues may also reflect coexisting and corresponding deficits. Though Ramban views Yosef's brave self-confidence as praiseworthy, Yosef may alternatively be seen as acting in a somewhat reckless, if not foolhardy, manner, displaying a stubborn self-assuredness in his cognitive abilities and a seeming compulsion to display his talents to others. Indeed, for individuals on the spectrum, strengths and weaknesses are not only compatible, but are often

When the *Sar HaMashkim* and the *Sar HaOphim* tell Yosef that they had dreams but do not have an interpreter,[10] Yosef responds immediately and with great authority, dominating and directing the rest of the conversation. Yosef the dreamer is now in his element, in the world of dreams, where he can confidently display his unique talents. Apparently without a moment's pause, Yosef tells them that God interprets dreams, and he requests that they describe what they have dreamt.[11]

When the *Sar HaMashkim* recounts his dream, Yosef replies:

> This is its meaning: . . . In three more days, Pharaoh will lift up your head and return you to your position. . . . Only if you will remember me . . . and you will recall me to Pharaoh and you will take me out of [prison]. Because I was kidnapped from the Land of the Hebrews and here too I have not done anything for which they placed me in prison.[12]

Upon hearing the dream of the *Sar HaMashkim*,[13] Yosef can hardly contain himself, not only interpreting the dream with great certainty[14] and specificity,[15] but also adding the request that the *Sar HaMashkim* remember him, recall him to Pharaoh, and have him taken out of prison.[16] Yosef further adds that he had been kidnapped from the Land of the *Ivrim* and that he was wrongfully imprisoned.[17]

Yosef's interpretation is impressive. Indeed, the *Sar HaOphim* recognizes the accuracy of Yosef's interpretation, because, as Rashbam explains, the truth is plainly recognized,[18] and Yosef's

---

inextricably linked.

10. 40:8.
11. 40:8.
12. 40: 12–15.
13. 40:9–11.
14. See 40:12 (Yosef states, categorically, "This is its meaning. . . .").
15. 40:12–13.
16. 40:14.
17. 40:15.
18. See Rashbam 40:16 (citing a Talmudic principle). See also Rabbi Samson Raphael Hirsch's Commentary on the Torah 40:16; Nechama Leibowitz, *Studies in Bereishis* (Hebrew) 302. Chizkuni suggests that the *Sar HaOphim* found Yosef's interpretation credible because it included a

interpretation is plainly true. However, like many on the spectrum, Yosef is so deeply absorbed in truth – his truth – that he fails to articulate this valuable information in a way that is consistent with socially acceptable norms. Thus, while Yosef succeeds in displaying his cognitive gifts, he again stumbles in his social interactions.

Rather than waiting for the *Sar HaMashkim* to acknowledge his brilliance, to absorb what he has said, and to offer to respond in kind to the good news he brings, Yosef immediately imposes upon the *Sar HaMashkim* – nearly demands of him[19] – to arrange to have Pharaoh free Yosef from prison. Surely, the *Sar HaMashkim* has more important priorities and interests in mind at this point. He is currently sitting in prison for the crime he has committed to Pharaoh, and like almost any prisoner, his primary concern is simply to escape his present fate.[20] Even if Yosef's interpretation does, in fact, come to fruition, and even if he remembers Yosef, the *Sar HaMashkim* will presumably be reluctant to expend his newly-found good will with Pharaoh in an effort to free Yosef.[21]

Yet, without missing a beat or allowing for a gradual and socially appropriate dialogue to develop, Yosef calls out his own desires, demands, and expectations, unable to picture the situation from someone else's perspective. Similar to his earlier interactions with his brothers and father, Yosef has already mapped out, in his own mind, the future that he forecasts for himself and the roles he envisions for others within his ambitious self-projection. Although in both cases he will ultimately be proven correct, and uncannily so, his ability to see the truth

---

concrete prediction of an imminent event that would occur in just three days, and it was therefore subject to falsification. See Chizkuni 40:16.

19. As Malbim observes, Yosef introduces his request with the conditional phrase *ki im*, possibly implying that his interpretation of the dream will come to fruition "only if" the *Sar HaMashkim* remembers him. See Malbim 40:14.

20. See *Meleches Machsheves* 40:5.

21. Moreover, even if the *Sar HaMashkim* asks Pharaoh for clemency in Yosef's behalf, it is far from certain that Pharaoh will grant his request. Yet, in Yosef's articulation of the events, the success of his plan seems a fait accompli: "You will recall me to Pharaoh and you will take me out" of prison. 40:14. Cf. Radak 40:14; Rashbam 40:14.

does not offset his inability to see the way his mannerisms appear to others and to appreciate the effect his actions will have on the way they respond to him.

Yosef also stumbles in the choice of information he asks the *Sar HaMashkim* to bring to Pharaoh's attention. First, he requests that the *Sar HaMashkim* "recall" him to Pharaoh, apparently referencing Yosef's familiarity to Pharaoh through his service in the house of Potiphar.[22] However, it was during this time of service to Potiphar that Yosef was found to have committed the crime for which he is presently imprisoned. It would seem counterproductive to remind Pharaoh of the site of Yosef's purported jailable offense, as part of a request that Yosef be freed from prison. In a later conversation with Pharaoh, the *Sar HaMashkim* is reluctant to recall his own past crime and delicately voices regret for having the need to do so.[23]

Second, Yosef adds – and apparently would like the *Sar HaMashkim* to tell Pharaoh – that he was kidnapped from the Land of the *Ivrim*.[24] Given the ostracism of the *Ivrim* in Egypt,[25] reminding Pharaoh of Yosef's lowly origins would likewise seem to cause more harm than any possible good.[26] Finally, Yosef declares that he has not done anything in Egypt for which he deserves to be in prison.[27] Despite Yosef's understandable desire to declare his own innocence – which also represents the truth – Yosef's denial of guilt will only serve as a further reminder of Potiphar's claim to the contrary. There is no reason to expect that Pharaoh will believe the self-serving

22. See Ramban 40:14; Sforno 40:14.

23. See Radak 41:9.

24. 40:15.

25. See Ramban 39:14; Abravanel 39:14.

26. Chizkuni cites the midrashic statement that because he identified himself as an *Ivri*, Yosef merited to be buried in the Land of Israel. See Chizkuni 40:15; *Torah Shelema* note [37]. Clearly, the midrash sees Yosef's open pride in his connection to the Land of the *Ivrim* as courageous and admirable. Yet again, though, through a different lens, Yosef may be seen as unable to recognize the possibly negative ramifications of having others associate him as an *Ivri*. In this view, Yosef may be exhibiting social naïveté rather than – or alongside with and as a complement to – his demonstration of brave strength.

27. 40:15.

protestations of the self-identified kidnapped *Ivri* in the face of the accusations levelled against him by Pharaoh's noble and trusted commissioner.

Though Yosef's request to the *Sar HaMashkim* thus seems misguided and impolitic, it makes complete sense in the world that Yosef inhabits within his own mind, the world of truth. In fact, all of Yosef's statements are objectively and eminently true: he served Potiphar faithfully and productively, he was the victim of a kidnapping from his home in the Land of the *Ivrim*, and he did not do anything wrong in Egypt to warrant imprisonment. Again, though, because he remains absorbed in his own world, Yosef fails to understand how to temper or articulate the truth in a way that will appeal to others.

Yosef demonstrates a similar combination of intellectual acumen and social ineptitude in his response to the *Sar HaOphim*, interpreting his dream with remarkable precision, but communicating the information in a highly unusual manner. The *Sar HaOphim* tells Yosef of his dream only after witnessing Yosef's indisputably accurate interpretation of the dream of the *Sar HaMashkim*,[28] which included the favorable prediction that "in three more days, Pharaoh will lift up your head and return you to your position. . . ."[29] Thus, the *Sar HaOphim* optimistically describes his own dream – which on the surface was quite similar to that of the *Sar HaMashkim* – presumably hoping for a similar interpretation.[30]

Yosef replies to the *Sar HaOphim* that "in three more days, Pharaoh will lift up your head from on you and hang you. . . ."[31] Juxtaposed with his prediction to the *Sar HaMashkim*, the phraseology of Yosef's response to the *Sar HaOphim* seems rather curious. In some ways, Yosef's wordplay may appear clever, but at the same time, to the *Sar HaOphim* – and possibly to the *Sar HaMashkim* – it probably sounded cruel. After all, upon hearing Yosef's opening words, identical to the start of the interpretation Yosef provided the *Sar HaMashkim*, the *Sar*

28. 40:16. See Rashbam 40:16.
29. 40:13.
30. See Ramban 40:16; Abravanel.
31. 40:19.

HaOphim must have anticipated that he was going to enjoy a similarly positive fate. However, his hopes were quickly dashed by Yosef's colorful turn of phrase, informing him, instead, of his impending doom.[32] Whatever Yosef's motivation, he conveyed the truth in a way that, in both form and substance, reflected his brilliance, but also in a manner that was surely devastating to the listener.[33]

As the episode concludes, the text relates that, after being reinstated in his position, the *Sar HaMashkim* "did not remember . . . Yosef" and "forgot him."[34] In addition to the apparent redundancy, the verse seems to beg the question as to why – and how – the *Sar HaMashkim* fails to remember Yosef, who just three days ago played such an important role in his life and passionately requested that he not be forgotten.[35]

While commentators offer various explanations to resolve both of these difficulties, perhaps the text may once again reveal aspects of Yosef's character by portraying the way others react to him. Though the *Sar HaMashkim* has encountered Yosef's brilliance, and may feel a sense of gratitude for his favorable interpretation of the dream, he has also witnessed Yosef's socially inept and off-putting behaviors. Thus, the apparent redundancy in the verse may indicate an inherent tension, a two-step process, which develops and gradually plays out in the mind of the *Sar HaMashkim*.

---

32. Rashbam notes the similarities in Yosef's phrasing of the two interpretations. See Rashbam 40:19. See also *Torah Shelema* [32] and note [32].

33. The text later states that Pharaoh "lifted up the head of the *Sar HaMashkim* and the head of the *Sar HaOphim* amongst his servants," 40:20, before detailing the very different fates that befell them. 40:21–22. Thus, in the context of an objective articulation of the events, the phrase "lifted up the head . . ." simply described Pharaoh's recalling the two servants from prison. Yosef, however, modified this objectively reasonable – and truthful – description and, in the context of his interpretation to the *Sar HaOphim*, altered the meaning of the phrase to deliver a truthful message in an unusual and insensitive manner.

34. 40:23.

35. Perhaps on account of this difficulty, *midrashim* describe various scenarios in which the *Sar HaMashkim* was planning to remember Yosef, but was prevented from doing so by Divine intervention. See *Torah Shelema* [52], [53], and notes [52], [53].

At first, perhaps the *Sar HaMashkim* is so overwhelmed by his sudden reversal of fortune and return to prominence that he initially – passively, and understandably – fails to remember Yosef.[36] However, after adjusting to the transition, the *Sar HaMashkim* would presumably have an opportunity to reflect upon his good fortune and to recall Yosef and his request. Yet, upon further reflection, he may also recall Yosef's socially inappropriate behaviors, and it may be no wonder that he makes the decision to distance himself from Yosef. Accordingly, the verse emphasizes, when he begins to remember Yosef, the *Sar HaMashkim* makes an effort to keep Yosef out of his memory, signified by the active form of the verb *va'yishkachehu* ("and he forgot him").[37] In short, notwithstanding Yosef's gifts, perhaps the *Sar HaMashkim* simply could not bring himself to plead with Pharaoh in behalf of someone with Yosef's social disabilities.[38]

Whatever the explanation for the inability or unwillingness of the *Sar HaMashkim* to remember Yosef, the conclusion of this episode tragically illustrates the extent and ramifications of Yosef's failure to navigate social settings to his own advantage. Even amidst his success, Yosef's social deficits prevent him from being able to elicit the kinship and support of someone who recognized and benefited from his remarkable talents. Instead of being freed immediately upon the reinstatement of the *Sar HaMashkim*, Yosef will remain imprisoned for two more years until, only as a last resort, when there will be no one else to interpret Pharaoh's dreams, the *Sar HaMashkim* will have no choice but to mention him to Pharaoh.[39]

---

36. 40:23 ("did not remember . . . Yosef").

37. 40:23. Cf. Rashi 40:23; Rashbam 40:23 (understanding the phrase "did not remember" as a reference to the day the *Sar HaMashkim* was released from prison, and the phrase "and he forgot" as a reference to a later time).

38. This reading is consistent with the interpretation of the *Sar HaMashkim*'s later confession to Pharaoh of his "sins," 41:9, as an allusion to his failure to remember Yosef, see *Torah Shelema* 41:9 [36] and note [36]; Chizkuni 41:9 – implying the *Sar HaMashkim*'s culpability, presumably for a conscious effort to forget Yosef.

39. According to Rashi and several *midrashim*, Yosef remains in prison for two additional years as a punishment for placing his trust in the *Sar*

HaMashkim rather than in God. See Rashi 40:23; *Torah Shelema* 40:14 note [33], 40:23 [54], 41:2 [3], [4].

An alternate midrash states that Yosef would have been imprisoned for only ten years, for speaking about his brothers to their father, but he was imprisoned for two additional years because of his request to the *Sar HaMashkim*. See *Torah Shelema* 40:14 [33]. Rather than faulting Yosef for a lack of trust in God when speaking with the *Sar HaMashkim*, this midrash draws a comparison to when Yosef spoke about his brothers, and seems to connect the consequences of his conduct in the two cases. Yet, this midrash does not identify the basis for the comparison or explain the underlying reason that Yosef's words to the *Sar HaMashkim* should result in his further imprisonment.

A number of commentators suggest that when Yosef spoke about his brothers, he did so without malicious intent. Rather, he observed – or perceived – that they had acted improperly, and in his zealous dedication to discover and reveal the truth, he felt compelled to bring their misdeeds to the attention of their father. See, e.g., Sforno 37:2; *Gur Aryeh* 37:2. Despite his good intentions, however, Yosef failed to recognize the impression that his words and actions would have on his brothers, and to anticipate the social ramifications of his conduct, which ultimately resulted in his sale and, later, his imprisonment in Egypt. Likewise, Yosef's wish that the *Sar HaMashkim* remember him seems fair and reasonable, and his request that the *Sar HaMashkim* return the favor is consistent with his sense of truth and justice. Here too, however, Yosef fails to realize that the socially awkward manner in which he makes the request will discourage the *Sar HaMashkim* from undertaking any efforts in his behalf. Accordingly, Yosef's actions will bring him two more years of imprisonment.

In this reading of the midrash, once again the misfortunes that befall Yosef may be viewed not as a form of Divine retribution for sinful conduct but as a natural consequence of his condition and his self-absorbed behaviors, which may be well-meaning and even inherently noble in nature, but do not fit within societal norms and expectations. If so, rather than ascribing blame, the midrash may instead be reflecting the dual-edged reality of Yosef's character and personality, which at times enable him to achieve great success but at other times work to his considerable detriment.

Chapter 7

The *Sar HaMashkim* and Pharaoh

> And it was, at the end of two years, and Pharaoh was dreaming. . . . And it was, in the morning. . . , and he called all of the magicians of Egypt and all of its wise men and Pharaoh told them his dream, but none interpreted them for Pharaoh. And the *Sar HaMashkim* said to Pharaoh, ". . . in the prison . . . there with us was a Hebrew child, a slave to the chief slaughterer . . . and he interpreted for us our dreams, each man. . . . And it was, that as he interpreted for us, so it occurred. . . ."[1]

Notwithstanding his reasons for hesitation, in addition to feeling a sense of gratitude to Yosef, it would seem to be in the *Sar HaMashkim*'s own self-interest to take the earliest opportunity to mention Yosef to Pharaoh. By bringing Yosef's undeniable brilliance to Pharaoh's attention, the *Sar HaMashkim* might hope to win for himself a measure of Pharaoh's appreciation, and possibly to be rewarded for his assistance. Moreover, when he hears that Pharaoh has had a strange dream and is seeking an interpretation,[2] the *Sar HaMashkim* would be expected to enthusiastically recommend that Yosef be called to exhibit his unique gift. In turn, the *Sar HaMashkim* might anticipate, when Yosef interprets the dream correctly, he will receive at least part of the credit.

Nevertheless, the *Sar HaMashkim* appears reluctant to talk about Yosef, and even when he decides that it is necessary to tell Pharaoh about Yosef's remarkable ability to interpret

1. 41:1, 8–10, 12, 13.
2. 41:8.

dreams, he uses a string of pejorative terms to describe Yosef: *na'ar*; *Ivri*; *eved* (child; Hebrew; slave).[3] This unusually negative characterization of the individual he is recommending to Pharaoh – presumably with the aim that Pharaoh will accept his recommendation – prompts the midrash to criticize the *Sar HaMashkim* as unable to be fully magnanimous even when assisting others.[4]

Perhaps, though, the *Sar HaMashkim*'s actions regarding Yosef tell us more about Yosef than about the *Sar HaMashkim*. Once again, the seemingly contradictory manner in which others interact with – or act toward – Yosef may reflect the contradictions they see within Yosef himself, which are commonly found in individuals who are on the spectrum. In particular, the *Sar HaMashkim*'s use of the term *na'ar*, to accompany his depiction of Yosef as an *eved* and an *Ivri*,[5] may be intended to signal to Pharaoh not a categorically negative depiction of Yosef, but a more nuanced and complex picture.

Although the text does not identify the crimes that the *Sar HaMashkim* and the *Sar HaOphim* committed against Pharaoh, commentators suggest relatively minor offenses involving a minimal breach of royal protocol.[6] As a consequence of these minor slights to the respect demanded by Pharaoh, the two servants were imprisoned, with the *Sar HaOphim* ultimately executed. Now that he is back in Pharaoh's court, the *Sar HaMashkim* is understandably reluctant to recommend that the King release from prison and seek the advice of an uncouth, erratic, and unpredictable *Ivri* – whose mention would also remind Pharaoh of the *Sar HaMashkim*'s own transgression.

It is only after Pharaoh has called upon all of the *chartumim* (magicians) and all of the *chachamim* (wise men) – to no avail[7] – that the *Sar HaMashkim* realizes he can no longer remain silent. At this point, it has become eminently and unavoidably clear that he must make mention of Yosef's uncanny ability

---

3. 41:12.
4. See *Torah Shelema* [39]; Rashi 41:12.
5. 41:12.
6. See *Torah Shelema* 40:1 [3]; Rashi 40:1; Chizkuni 40:1.
7. 41:8.

to correctly interpret dreams. Even now, though, the *Sar HaMashkim* is nervous about the prospect of having Yosef appear before Pharaoh. He recalls vividly that Yosef's ingenious interpretation of the previous dreams was accompanied by socially inappropriate and somewhat bizarre behaviors. The *Sar HaMashkim* continues to fear that, in the course of interpreting Pharaoh's dream, Yosef will likewise engage in behaviors that, at the very least, are unfit for the presence of the King. As the *Sar HaMashkim* well knows from his own narrow escape, this kind of conduct will not be tolerated, and he worries that it can carry serious consequences for both Yosef and himself.

Therefore, when the *Sar HaMashkim* finally feels compelled to mention Yosef to Pharaoh, he does so in a rather unusual manner, referring to Yosef as a *na'ar Ivri, eved. . . .*[8] As *midrashim* and commentators observe, the terms *Ivri* and *eved* are allusions to Yosef's status as an outsider.[9] In an earlier episode, Potiphar's wife had used similar terms to portray Yosef as a stranger, in a way that suited her own insidious purposes.[10] For the *Sar HaMashkim,* depicting Yosef as an outsider serves the purpose of alleviating any of Pharaoh's potential concerns that Yosef might have aspirations of grandeur, while at the same time deflecting any criticism the *Sar HaMashkim* may face for his delay in mentioning Yosef's abilities.[11]

In contrast to Potiphar's wife, however, the *Sar HaMashkim* adds the term *na'ar,* which seems peculiar and out of place in the context of recommending a wise man who has the talents to provide heroic counsel to Pharaoh. Commentators note the anomaly of earlier references to the teenage Yosef as a *na'ar,* prompting some to infer that, although he was intellectually advanced, Yosef displayed behaviors of a younger child.[12] Many years later, the *Sar HaMashkim* describes the adult Yosef as a *na'ar,* perhaps signaling to Pharaoh that despite Yosef's un-

---

8. 41:12.

9. See *Torah Shelema* [39]; Rashi 41:12; Chizkuni 41:12. See also Ramban 39:14; Abravanel 39:14.

10. See 39:14, 17.

11. See Rashi 41:12; Chizkuni 41:12.

12. See *Torah Shelema* 37:2 [33]; Rashi 37:2; Sforno 37:2; *Gur Aryeh* 37:2; *Michtav M'Eliyahu* 227–29.

deniable brilliance, Pharaoh should be aware of the deficits in Yosef's social development, which may be exhibited in unfortunate and inappropriate behaviors.

Drawing from a midrash, Rashi explains that the *Sar HaMashkim* uses the label *na'ar* to connote that Yosef is a *shoteh* (a fool),[13] which, according to Rashi, implies that Yosef is not worthy of greatness.[14] Notably, however, a close reading of the *midrashim* may suggest an understanding – or an emphasis – somewhat different from Rashi's. Specifically, unlike Rashi, *Midrash Rabbah* simply refers to Yosef as a *shoteh,* without further explication,[15] while *Midrash Tanchuma* adds that Yosef is not a *bar da'at* (a person with wisdom).[16]

At first glance, midrashic references to Yosef as a *shoteh* and bereft of *da'at* seem even more surprising than the verse's use of the term *na'ar.* After all, whatever the explanation for the *Sar HaMashkim*'s decision to demean Yosef in Pharaoh's eyes by using derogatory language, it would seem downright counterproductive for him to minimize or degrade Yosef's wisdom during the course of his attempt to convince Pharaoh to call upon Yosef's unparalleled ability to interpret dreams.

Perhaps, though, the *midrashim* employ the concepts of *shoteh* and lacking *da'at* advisedly, suggesting that the *Sar HaMashkim* uses the term *na'ar* to indicate a very specific quality in Yosef. The term *shoteh,* like the term *na'ar,* may be intended to imply that Yosef is, at once, both intellectually brilliant and socially inappropriate, if not somewhat deranged, in his behaviors.[17] Although he has concluded that he has no choice

13. See *Torah Shelema* [39]; Rashi 41:12.

14. See Rashi 41:12.

15. See *Torah Shelema* [39].

16. See *Torah Shelema* note [39].

17. Perhaps this is the meaning of the word *shoteh* as used in the midrashic interpretation of the verse describing Shlomo (Solomon) as wiser than anyone else. I Kings 5:11. See also *Kobetz HeAros* 271. The midrash understands this verse as emphasizing that Shlomo was wiser *afilu min hashotim,* possibly indicating that the term *shoteh* connotes a degree of wisdom or brilliance, along with the more common connotation of a form of derangement.

Notably, in halachic contexts, a *shoteh* is characterized primarily on the basis of aberrant behaviors, see Talmud Bavli, Chagigah 3b–4a, or a single

but to recommend Yosef to Pharaoh, the *Sar HaMashkim* has witnessed Yosef's strange behaviors in the past, and he wants to be sure to caution Pharaoh about the possibility of a recurrence. Likewise, the notion that Yosef lacks *da'at* may refer not to Yosef's cognitive capacity, but to his inability to regulate his behaviors to match his intellectual prowess.

Thus, just as there was no contradiction between earlier references to Yosef as both a gifted *ben zekunim* and a socially inept *na'ar*, the *Sar HaMashkim* depicts Yosef in a way that reflects this complex reality, common to individuals on the spectrum. Accordingly, describing Yosef as a *na'ar* serves as both a warning to Pharaoh, to be prepared to encounter possibly strange behaviors – albeit coupled with brilliant insights, and as a further explanation as to why the *Sar HaMashkim* hesitated before recommending Yosef to him.

Individuals on the spectrum, their family, and their friends often confront an uneasy balance between the desire to allow these individuals to fully engage society and proudly display their talents and abilities, weighed against the fears that their social miscues will lead others to marginalize and reject them. As a result, such individuals sometimes miss opportunities to enter settings where they would otherwise thrive, due to an overriding concern for the way they will be perceived by those who are too intolerant or insecure to accept them as they are.

The *Sar HaMashkim*'s reluctance – and near refusal – to mention Yosef to Pharaoh illustrates the potentially tenuous nature of success for otherwise highly qualified individuals on the spectrum. Projecting his own fears onto Pharaoh, the *Sar HaMashkim* initially tries to avoid re-engaging or remembering Yosef. When he has no choice but to recall Yosef's abilities, he does so in a way that continues to reflect and express his doubts and concerns about Yosef's behaviors. Ironically, though, his fears are unfounded, as Pharaoh not only disregards his warning, but demonstrates a willingness to fully overlook Yosef's social deficits, in favor of developing and exploiting his talents.

---

cognitive aberration, even in the absence of any other cognitive deficits. See Rambam, Mishneh Torah, Laws of *Edut* 9:9.

Chapter 8

Yosef and Pharaoh

> And Pharaoh sent and called for Yosef, and they quickly retrieved him from prison, and he shaved and changed his clothes and came before Pharaoh. And Pharaoh said to Yosef, "I dreamt a dream and there is no interpreter of it, and I heard about you that you can hear a dream to interpret it." And Yosef answered to Pharaoh, "It lies beyond me, God will answer Pharaoh's peace." And Pharaoh said to Yosef, "In my dream. . . ."[1]

Yosef's interactions with Pharaoh are likewise telling in what they say about Yosef, both directly, through Yosef's behaviors, and indirectly, through the way Pharaoh reacts to him. Unlike the *Sar HaMashkim*, who was worried that Yosef might engage in erratic and eccentric breaches of royal protocol, Pharaoh remains undeterred and, initially, undisturbed by Yosef's supposed lack of social graces. When Pharaoh hears about Yosef's skills, he ignores the *Sar HaMashkim*'s pejorative descriptions and implicit warnings. Instead, he immediately calls for Yosef, who is quickly taken from prison, appropriately groomed and dressed, and brought before the King.[2]

When Yosef appears, Pharaoh is deferential and encouraging,[3] playing to Yosef's strengths by articulating his own needs and his awareness of Yosef's ability to interpret dreams.[4] To

1. 41:14–17.
2. 41:14.
3. See *Meleches Machsheves* 44:18.
4. 41:15.

survive and succeed as King, Pharaoh, like many leaders, presumably has to possess the wherewithal to find the strengths in others and identify the value they may bring to the kingdom, while at the same time recognizing and, when necessary, accommodating their deficits and weaknesses.

Yosef replies that it lies beyond him, that God will answer Pharaoh.[5] Although Yosef's modesty is admirable, the wisdom of his response is questionable. After all, Pharaoh has just retrieved him from prison because of his acumen in interpreting dreams. As such, Yosef should not downplay his own talents, and his first words to Pharaoh should certainly not dispute Pharaoh's generous introductory remarks.[6] Moreover, Yosef seems overconfident in asserting that God will answer Pharaoh, when he has not yet heard the substance of the dream. Finally, invoking God to Pharaoh seems to repeat Yosef's past errors, serving again as a reminder of Yosef's status as an *Ivri*.

In fact, Yosef need not have offered any reply to Pharaoh at this point. Pharaoh's initial remarks, signaled by the relatively benign *va'yomer* ("and he said"),[7] were likely intended as a way to break the ice and to make Yosef feel comfortable in his new surroundings. Yosef's response, in contrast, is preceded by *va'ya'an* ("and he answered"),[8] because he is answering Pharaoh – actually, contradicting and correcting him – even though Pharaoh was not asking any questions.[9] Apparently out of his commitment to speak the truth, Yosef feels compelled to interrupt the pleasantries of their opening conversation by correcting Pharaoh. As the *Sar HaMashkim* had anticipated, Yosef is immediately exhibiting socially inappropriate behavior. He does not think of how his actions impact others – even Pharaoh – or the detrimental effects they may have on himself.

Pharaoh's next statement is prefaced with the more pointed *va'yedaber* ("and he spoke"),[10] as he seemingly begins to feel a bit irritated by Yosef. Nevertheless, Pharaoh does not allow himself

5. 41:16.
6. See *Michtav M'Eliyahu* 4:30.
7. 41:15.
8. 41:16.
9. Cf. Abravanel.
10. 41:17.

to become overly concerned with Yosef's behaviors, recognizing the overriding value of Yosef's brilliance. At the same time, Pharaoh realizes that when interacting with Yosef, he should dispense with small talk and social courtesies. Accordingly, he gets down to business and, without further ado, immediately launches into a detailed description of his dreams.[11]

Alternatively, Josephus understands Pharaoh's opening statement to Yosef as a request that Yosef have the courage to tell him the unvarnished truth, and not simply recite what he thinks Pharaoh would like to hear.[12] Indeed, it is not clear why none of the *chachamim* or *chartumim* in the land were able to provide a suitable interpretation of Pharaoh's dream, and the Torah does not relate the substance of any of their suggestions. Perhaps the candid and blunt nature of Yosef's advice indicates that the others failed because they were reluctant to tell Pharaoh the bitter truth, that he would face the challenge of years of famine.[13] Just as the *Sar HaMashkim* was understandably fearful to cause even the slightest breach of protocol toward the King, Pharaoh's advisers were fearful to convey any negative messages present in the dreams.

If so, Pharaoh may have found Yosef's transparency to be a

11. 41:17–41:24.

12. See Da'at Mikra / Mossad Harav Kook 41:16 (citing Josephus). See also *Kli Yakar* 41:8.

13. This reading might provide further insight into Pharaoh's enthusiastic reaction to the *Sar HaMashkim*'s otherwise lukewarm recommendation of Yosef. Notably, the *Sar HaMashkim* mentions not only his own dream and the positive interpretations and events that ensued, but also the dream – and execution – of the *Sar HaOphim*. 41:13. Immediately thereafter, without so much as a word to the *Sar HaMashkim*, Pharaoh sends for Yosef. 41:14. Perhaps Pharaoh is pleased to hear of Yosef's willingness to provide a negative interpretation to the *Sar HaOphim*, thus demonstrating his courage and ability to provide Pharaoh with a candid interpretation. Cf. *Meshech Chochma* 40:2.

Likewise, this reading might explain why Yosef offers a description of the years of famine before describing the years of plenty, contrary to the order of the dream and to the chronological order of the events. See Ramban 41:27; Chizkuni 41:27. Yosef wanted to emphasize the uncomfortable truth, establishing his credibility in Pharaoh's eyes and thereby reassuring Pharaoh of the accuracy of the positive interpretation and encouraging advice he would also provide.

welcome and refreshing change, in both form and substance, compared with the cautious platitudes he repeatedly heard from the "yes-men" who advised him. In this reading, perhaps Pharaoh's opening remarks to Yosef were intended as a test, to see if Yosef's response would differ from the bland and prosaic manner of all those who failed to provide convincing interpretations of the dreams. Yosef immediately passes the test when he demonstrates his willingness to correct and contradict Pharaoh as necessary. Having been thereby assured of Yosef's courage and candor, Pharaoh begins to describe his dreams, without further delay.[14]

Thus, Yosef's dedication to the truth, which in other contexts proved dangerous and detrimental, serves him well in his interactions with Pharaoh. Conversely, Pharaoh benefits from his willingness and ability to overlook Yosef's deficits and to exploit his talents, for his own purposes. For individuals on the spectrum to succeed, is it often necessary for those in a position of power and authority to be willing and able – whether out of kindness or out of self-interest – to see past deficits, disabilities, and developmental delays, and instead to identity and cultivate skills and talents that can be mutually beneficial to all involved.

In any event, when Pharaoh completes his description of the dreams, Yosef returns to the same pattern of behavior that characterized many of his earlier interactions. Yosef carefully analyzes Pharaoh's dream, brilliantly explaining the symbolism of each detail in a way that also reveals the meaning of the dream as a whole.[15] However, once again, though the substance of Yosef's disquisition is an expression of utter genius, the manner in which he responds to Pharaoh betrays a failure to comply

14. Perhaps along these lines, when Pharaoh later appoints Yosef to a position of power, beyond all others in the kingdom, he notably uses the term *u'vil'adecha*, 41:44, echoing Yosef's use of the term *u'vil'aday* in his declaration that the interpretation of Pharaoh's dream lies beyond him. 41:16. Although the midrash seems to understand the parallel language as an indication of Divine reward for Yosef's humble glorification of the honor of God, see *Torah Shelema* [104], on a human level, Pharaoh may be signaling his approval of Yosef's willingness and ability to assert his candid opinion and stand his ground in the face of opposing views.

15. 41:25–37.

with social convention, particularly as befits the presence of the King.

Two aspects of Yosef's monologue are particularly striking. First, in the course of his analysis, Yosef references God three more times.[16] As he did with Potiphar's wife and the *Sar HaMashkim*, as well as during his introduction to Pharaoh, Yosef thereby reminds his inquisitor of his own status as a member of the hated *Ivri* nation, which worships a foreign and unknown deity.

Second, after he has completed his interpretation of Pharaoh's dream, Yosef does not stop speaking, but instead he continues with instructions on what course of action Pharaoh should take pursuant to the interpretation.[17] Commentators observe the apparent hubris of Yosef, who has been released from prison for the express and limited purpose of interpreting Pharaoh's dream, yet takes it upon himself to advise – essentially to order – Pharaoh how to proceed over the next fourteen years.[18] Repeating the mode of his encounter with the *Sar HaMashkim*, after providing information – brilliant, accurate information – Yosef does not wait for a response or allow the information to sink in. Eschewing the ordinary give and take of appropriate interpersonal dialogue, Yosef jumps ahead to the next step of his own thought process, without considering the perspective of his listener. While this behavior was unfortunate during Yosef's conversation with the *Sar HaMashkim*, it seems downright reckless when directed toward Pharaoh.

Moreover, although Yosef's request that the *Sar HaMashkim* remember him may have been a bit forward and even misguided, Yosef couched his request in terms of *na* – asking that the *Sar HaMashkim* "please" perform a kindness for him.[19] And yet, Yosef's unconventional behaviors nearly caused the *Sar HaMashkim* to reject his request, at all costs. Here, Yosef issues instructions to Pharaoh, prefaced with *v'ata* ("and now"),[20] and

16. 41:25; 41:28; 41:32.

17. 41:33–36.

18. See Ramban 41:33; *Meleches Machsheves* 41:33; *HaK'sav V'haKabbala* 41:33; Nechama Leibowitz, *Studies in Bereishis* (Hebrew) 313–18.

19. See Rashi 40:14.

20. See Nechama Leibowitz, *Studies in Bereishis* (Hebrew) 315 and

he continues to frame his ideas in the form of virtually imperative commands to the King. Finally, as Ramban notes, Yosef advises Pharaoh to appoint a wise man to administer his plan, implicitly nominating himself – not very subtly – to be considered for the position.[21]

Unlike the *Sar HaMashkim*, however, Pharaoh does not recoil from Yosef. To attain and hold onto his power, Pharaoh has likely developed the ability to quickly take the measure of others, and to focus on finding a role for them in support of his own ambitions.[22] He immediately grasps that Yosef has displayed undeniable genius, in both his interpretation of the dream and his detailed plan for ensuring Egypt's continued vitality and prosperity.

Indeed, Yosef's brilliance is plain for all to see. Even Pharaoh's servants, who have failed in their own attempts to provide the correct interpretation of Pharaoh's dreams and probably resent Yosef, recognize the accuracy of his interpretation and the wisdom of his plans.[23] At the same time, Yosef's strange conduct is likewise undeniable, presumably prompting surprise – or disdain – among Pharaoh's servants. They see him as an uncouth *Ivri*,[24] who is unable to comply with the protocol that is demanded before Pharaoh and unable to stop himself from

---

note 4.

21. See Ramban 41:33.

22. For example, *Meshech Chochma* explains that in appointing Yosef, Pharaoh saw an opportunity to bolster his own exalted image in the eyes of the nation, who would continue to view him as a deity, while Yosef would bear the burden of dealing with the mundane details of governing. See *Meshech Chochma* 41:33, 37. Indeed, when the famine begins and the nation cries out to Pharaoh, he immediately deflects responsibility by sending them to Yosef for instructions. See 41:55; Abravanel 41:54. Cf. *Meleches Machsheves* 39:22 (explaining that, in appointing Yosef as a leader, the *Sar Beit HaSohar* saw an opportunity to avoid the difficult and dangerous task of watching over the prisoners).

In a similar vein, according to Rabbi Yosef Dov Soloveitchik (cited in the ArtScroll *Chumash*), when Pharaoh later graciously arranges for all of Yosef's family to settle in Egypt, 45:17–20, he is motivated by his expectation that, like Yosef, they will bring skills and talents that will benefit the kingdom.

23. 41:37.

24. See Ramban 41:38.

repeatedly mentioning his God. Although Yosef's *davar* (statement)[25] "was good . . . in the eyes of all of [Pharaoh's] servants,"[26] the text does not relate that Yosef himself found favor in their eyes. They accept his brilliance but not him.

> And Pharaoh said to his servants, "Can we find like this, a man who has the spirit of God in him?" And Pharaoh said to Yosef, "Since God has told you all this, there is no one as discerning and wise like you. You will rule over my palace. . . ." And Pharaoh said to Yosef, "Look, I have placed you over all of the Land of Egypt." . . . [And Pharaoh] . . . dressed him in [royal garb] . . . . And Pharaoh said to Yosef, "I am Pharaoh, and beyond you, no one will raise his hand or leg in all of the Land of Egypt." And Pharaoh called Yosef *Tzafnat Pane'ach* (Zaphenath-Paneah) and he gave to him Osnat (Asenath), the daughter of Potiphera, the priest of On, as a wife . . . . And Yosef went out from before Pharaoh and passed through all of the Land of Egypt.[27]

Pharaoh understands his servants' reaction, but unlike the *Sar HaMashkim*, he does not have the option of forgetting Yosef. Pharaoh knows that he needs Yosef for his own purposes, and so, as Ramban notes, he has to find a way to convince his skeptical servants that Yosef is worthy of appointment to a position of high authority.[28] Thus, Pharaoh responds to his servants' unstated disdain for Yosef in a way that both defuses their concerns and turns Yosef's weaknesses into an apparent source of strength. Rather than ignoring Yosef's behaviors and his references to his God, with the hope that the servants will overlook these social deficits, Pharaoh embraces Yosef's differences. He asks his servants, rhetorically, whether another person can be found who possesses the same spirit of God.[29] As Ramban suggests, Pharaoh is explaining to his servants that it is necessary

25. See Onkelos 41:37.
26. 41:37.
27. 41:38–42, 44–46.
28. See Ramban 41:38.
29. 41:38.

for him to appoint Yosef because there is no one else like him among the Egyptians.[30]

Of course, the servants already know that Yosef is different. Repeating the pattern of Yosef's youth, his differences set him apart from them and prompt their contempt. However, Pharaoh's approach stands in stark contrast to Yaakov's actions. Yaakov first highlighted Yosef's special nature, giving him the coat of colors, only to unwittingly increase the brothers' hatred of the immature dreamer whose differences had already annoyed them. Yaakov then tried to integrate and ingratiate Yosef with his brothers, sending him on a mission that seemed doomed from the outset – and which failed miserably – because Yaakov did not see Yosef's differences the same way they were perceived by his peers.

Pharaoh realizes that Yosef will never be the same as the others, and so rather than trying to manufacture a plan to encourage his Egyptian servants to accept Yosef as one of their own, Pharaoh emphasizes Yosef's differences in a manner that will not bring about competition or jealousy. Instead, consistent with the servants' own impressions of Yosef, Pharaoh finds a way for them to accept Yosef as he is, in the role of the intellectual and social outsider, by virtue of his unique spiritual connection with the *Ivri* God.[31]

It is not uncommon for authority figures to try to integrate individuals on the spectrum through a method that attempts to minimize, conceal, or deny their differences, with the hope that their peers will ignore or fail to discover some of their otherwise hidden disabilities. Like Yaakov, however, parents, teachers, and others who employ these methods are often unsuccessful. If anything, it is nearly inevitable that at some point individuals on the spectrum will exhibit behaviors that will make their differences quite clear to their peers, who in

30. See Ramban 41:38.

31. See Ramban 41:38. Likewise, Abravanel observes that, in praising Yosef to his servants, Pharaoh focuses exclusively on Yosef's spiritual connection to God, which is unique to Yosef, rather than referring to Yosef's wisdom, which might be found among others in Egypt. In addition, Pharaoh may take care to refer to Yosef as an *ish,* 41:38, to emphasize that, although Yosef's behaviors are those of a *na'ar,* his wisdom befits an *ish.*

turn may resent these attempts, breeding not only their frustration toward the authority figure, but possibly their further anger toward the victim. Pharaoh's approach may be preferable, demonstrating that differences between individuals should be accepted, if not embraced, and that, at times, these differences are accompanied by different skills and talents, which should be recognized and welcomed.[32]

Having effectively and summarily allayed his servants' concerns about Yosef, Pharaoh immediately commences with Yosef's installation as viceroy of Egypt. Pharaoh now speaks directly to Yosef, informing him that because no one else is as wise as Yosef, he will rule over Pharaoh's palace.[33] Though Yosef does not respond, the text continues with an apparent non-sequitur, repeating "And Pharaoh said to Yosef . . ." to introduce Pharaoh's somewhat repetitive statement: "Look, I have placed you over all of the Land of Egypt."[34] One commentator suggests that Yosef was stunned by his sudden rise to power, accompanied by Pharaoh's abrupt and seemingly exaggerated reference to his unparalleled wisdom.[35] According to this explanation, Yosef thought Pharaoh might be joking, even mocking Yosef's earlier advice that Pharaoh select a "wise" person to lead the nation through the approaching years of feast and famine.[36] When Pharaoh observed Yosef's confused reaction, he began

---

32. Of course, as King, Pharaoh has a degree of power over his servants that is stronger than Yaakov's paternal authority over his children. Still, Ramban and others are sensitive to the need for even a king to win the approval of his subjects. See Ramban 41:38. Indeed, those in a position of authority – whether kings, employers, teachers, or parents – often face a somewhat similar task of understanding and managing not only the relative status, but also the social relationships, of those subject to their authority. In Pharaoh's case, the momentous decision to appoint Yosef requires this kind of social intelligence and management. Cf. *Beis Halevi*, Shemos (Exodus) 1:9–11 (explaining that Pharaoh had to convince his advisers that he was justified in enslaving the Nation of Israel).

33. 41:39–40.

34. See 41:41; Abravanel; Nechama Leibowitz, *Studies in Bereishis* (Hebrew) 317–18 note 7. Cf. Abravanel, Bamidbar (Numbers) 32:2–5.

35. See *Midreshei Hatorah*, cited in Nechama Leibowitz, *Studies in Bereishis* (Hebrew) 317–18.

36. See 41:33; *Midreshei Hatorah*, cited in Nechama Leibowitz, *Studies in Bereishis* (Hebrew) 317–18.

to speak again, redirecting and refocusing Yosef by instructing him somewhat firmly: "Look" or "Behold, I have placed you over all of the Land of Egypt."[37]

Notably, when he initially praises Yosef to the servants, in place of an affirmative endorsement, Pharaoh asks a rhetorical question: "Can we find like this, a man who has the spirit of God in him?"[38] Perhaps Yosef's confusion was the result of his inability, once again, to understand the subtle messages latent in the words of a speaker, conveyed through nonverbal cues, such as body language, or other forms of communication, such as tone of voice or inflection, which would imply sarcasm or a rhetorical question. Like many individuals on the spectrum, Yosef may have ascribed overly literal meanings to otherwise complex statements.

Thus, just as Yosef might have misunderstood his brothers' sarcasm, believing that they were confirming his ambitions of grandeur,[39] he might misunderstand Pharaoh's rhetorical question to be an affirmative command to his servants: "Let us find like this, a man who has the spirit of God in him." If so, Yosef would be utterly befuddled when, without waiting for such a search, Pharaoh abruptly turns to him and states that there is no one else with his degree of wisdom. Seeing this confusion, Pharaoh has to speak to Yosef afresh, firmly and directly, in a way that will dispel any doubts on Yosef's part and demonstrate the earnestness of his appointment.

Next, Pharaoh presents Yosef to the rest of the kingdom, dressing him in royal clothes and jewelry, and placing him in the royal chariot, to be led by servants announcing his appointment.[40] Commentators explain that Pharaoh has designed these public ceremonies as a means of reassuring the Egyptians of Yosef's fitness to serve as their leader, despite his *Ivri* heritage and his recent past as a prisoner.[41] Yet, during the course all of these events, Yosef still does not respond to Pharaoh.

---

37. See 41:41; *Midreshei Hatorah*, cited in Nechama Leibowitz, *Studies in Bereishis* (Hebrew) 317–18.

38. 41:38.

39. See 37:8.

40. 41:42–44.

41. See Radak 41:43; Abravanel; *HaK'sav V'haKabbala* 41:43.

Instead, Pharaoh again addresses Yosef, using the unusual introduction, "I am Pharaoh," followed by the declaration that no one else in the land will exercise any power over Yosef.[42] According to Abravanel, Pharaoh intends to send a message not to the Egyptians but to Yosef himself, assuring him that he will not experience the kind of jealousy that he encountered at the hands of his brothers.[43] Toward that end, Pharaoh sends word among both the nobility and the masses that Yosef will be afforded protection under royal authority.[44]

In this view, Pharaoh seems to compare favorably to Yaakov in his ability to anticipate, and take measures to deter, the potential hostility that Yosef's preferential treatment might bring about in others. In addition, in contrast to Yaakov, who relied on Yosef himself to tell his brothers that their father had sent him, Pharaoh employs royal messengers to insure that his decree is clearly delivered and received.

As an alternative explanation for Pharaoh's repeated declarations to Yosef, perhaps when Yosef hears of his appointment, he feels neither confusion nor fear, but a sense of self-satisfied gratification. Like many on the spectrum, in his younger years Yosef had perseverated, in self-absorption, on his dreams and visions for the future. Now, as he sees that his ambitions seem to be coming to fruition, he instinctively returns to the dreamlike state that had captured him as a teenager. Indeed, a similar dynamic appears to have accompanied Yosef's earlier success, both in the house of Potiphar, where he reverted to his childish behavior of twirling his hair, tending to his eyes, and lifting his heels,[45] and in prison, where he delivered his brilliant interpretations of the dreams, but in a manner that led the *Sar HaMashkim* to depict him as a *na'ar*.[46]

Accordingly, Pharaoh finds it necessary to repeatedly redirect and refocus Yosef, to return him to the task at hand. After addressing Yosef twice,[47] the second time with the firm

42. 41:44.
43. See Abravanel.
44. See Abravanel.
45. See 39:6; *Torah Shelema* [44].
46. 41:12.
47. 41:39; 41:41. As a corollary to this reading, perhaps Yosef, like many

instruction, "Look . . .,"[48] Pharaoh realizes that he has to go a step further. To break Yosef out of his dreamlike state, Pharaoh dresses him in royal clothes and surrounds him with the accoutrements of authority,[49] perhaps to impress upon Yosef the magnitude of his new role and his vast responsibilities. Still, observing Yosef's continuous lack of resolve, Pharaoh finally has to bring him back to the present reality by reminding him abruptly, "I am Pharaoh," and emphasizing, plainly and directly, that Yosef's authority will extend to such a degree that everyone in the land will be subject to his commands.[50]

In addition, Pharaoh realizes that, given Yosef's self-absorption, his lack of social skills, and his inability to navigate social challenges, Yosef is vulnerable to the maneuverings of those who are more clever, cunning, and calculating. Pharaoh has maintained power through shrewd utilization of his formidable political savvy, but Yosef is particularly ill-suited to deal with the bare-knuckled world of politics and the sharks who will be looking for every opportunity to hurt him – and possibly, by extension, cause harm to Pharaoh himself. Pharaoh preempts these threats by giving Yosef a new and honorable name[51] – and with it a new persona – as well as a wife, who can help protect him from the attacks and advances of others.[52] Significantly, Pharaoh selects a woman who is from a distinguished family – possibly the family of Potiphar[53] – who not only bestows further honor on Yosef by virtue of her pedigree, but who is presumably familiar with the intrigue and machinations of royal politics, and along with her family will be able to anticipate and help ward off challenges to Yosef.[54] With these supports

on the spectrum, has difficulty making eye contact with others, even – or particularly – when he is participating in conversations involving deep thought and emotion. Thus, Pharaoh uses phrases intended to direct Yosef to focus on Pharaoh's face and look him straight in the eye: "Look . . ."; "I am Pharaoh."

48. 41:41.
49. 41:42–43.
50. 41:44.
51. See 41:45; Ramban 41:45; Abravanel.
52. See Abravanel.
53. See Rashi 41:45.
54. See Abravanel; *Meshech Chochma* 41:45.

in place, Yosef is finally safe to go out on his own, leaving the protective watch of Pharaoh[55] and traveling throughout the Land of Egypt.[56]

It is not uncommon for individuals with disabilities, once they receive the appropriate services, structure, and supports, to be able to exercise the talents they possess and achieve the goals that would otherwise continue to elude them. As Pharaoh recognizes, like many who are on the spectrum, Yosef's deficits are in areas relating to social expectations and interactions.[57] To accommodate these deficits, Pharaoh provides Yosef with dignified clothes,[58] an honorable name,[59] servants,[60] and a wife to protect him and help him navigate his social surrounding.[61] Unencumbered by these external concerns, Yosef is now free to focus on his areas of strength, traveling throughout the Land of Egypt to construct and implement his masterful plan.[62] Again, Pharaoh appears to take a more effective course of action than Yaakov, who had similarly attempted to develop Yosef's talents,

55. 41:46. Cf. Radak 41:46; Abravanel. See also *HaK'sav V'haKabbala* 41:45.

56. 41:46.

57. See *Michtav M'Eliyahu* 2:229.

58. 41:22. This episode marks the second time Yosef has been provided by Pharaoh with a new set of clothes, see 41:14, in addition to the coat that Yaakov had given him. See 37:3. Of course, it is not surprising that Yosef needed new clothes, as well as a shave or haircut, when he was taken from prison to appear before Pharaoh, see 41:14, though notably, the text does not describe any such provisions for the *Sar HaMashkim* when he emerges from prison. Yosef's repeated need for others to provide him with different clothes, and his need to be provided a shave, see Ibn Ezra 41:14, may evoke a characteristic common among individuals on the spectrum to have challenges in various areas of personal grooming and appearance – particularly in matters dependent on social fashions and mores, such as styles of clothing and hairstyles. Similarly, Yosef's need to be provided a wife, who has the strength and status to protect him from others, see Abravanel; *Meshech Chochma* 41:45, may reflect aspects of social awkwardness and vulnerability, particularly in intimate relationships, common among individuals on the spectrum – as exemplified by Yosef's nearly catastrophic encounter with Potiphar's wife.

59. 41:45.

60. 41:43.

61. 41:45. See Abravanel.

62. 41:46–49.

but had fatefully sent Yosef out on his own without providing the necessary supports.

When Yosef has children, he gives them names that express his appreciation for his current good fortune, which overshadows and seems to help him forget the previous hardships he had suffered in his father's house and in Egypt.[63] Notably, Sforno draws a parallel between Yosef's feelings and Isaiah's depiction of messianic times, when earlier hardships will be forgotten.[64] Messianic times are characterized in Psalms as dreamlike – *hayinu k'cholmim* ("we were like dreamers")[65] – indicating that the future paradise will seem like a dream, or, alternatively, that the bitter past will disappear and, in retrospect, will feel as if it had been but a dream.[66] Yosef is now, in many ways, both living out his childhood dreams and leaving behind the earlier unpleasantness. This time, however, rather than reverting to an immature, self-absorbed, and self-detrimental dreamlike state, with the supports provided by Pharaoh, Yosef is in a position to make his dreams a reality, thereby setting the stage for his further success.

Thus, when the famine begins and the nation complains, Pharaoh confidently sends them directly to Yosef.[67] During the years of plenty, Yosef had divided the land into segments, gathering, storing, and allocating portions from among the abundant agricultural bounty.[68] Given the appearance, at that time, of a never-ending supply,[69] Yosef's decision to store substantial reserves may have seemed odd, and, as the midrash suggests, may have prompted reactions of doubt or even mockery,[70] but Pharaoh trusted him implicitly. Now, in times of famine, Yosef is proven correct and Pharaoh's trust in him is borne out, as

63. 41:50–52.
64. See Sforno 41:51 (quoting Isaiah 65:16).
65. Psalms 126:1.
66. See *Chidushei Maran Ri'z haLevi,* Psalms 126:1.
67. 41:54–55.
68. 41:47–49.
69. 41:49.
70. See *Torah Shelema* [121] and note [120].

Yosef has stored sufficient provisions to feed both the Egyptians and those arriving from surrounding lands.[71]

Significantly, during these years, Yosef continues to display some of the same qualities that, in the past, had proven detrimental to his interactions with others and had impeded his prospects of success. Yosef remains stubbornly absorbed in his own ideas and determined to follow the plan he has set out for himself and for Egypt, undeterred by – and appearing to be blithely unaware of – the dissent and mockery expressed towards his visions and actions. Yet, in a striking reversal of his previous behaviors, Yosef is no longer an impetuous and oblivious *na'ar* who fails to contemplate the long-term consequences of his impulsive conduct. To the contrary, with Pharaoh's guidance and support, Yosef has matured to the degree that he now anticipates future needs, and he acts accordingly to insure the prosperity of Egypt and its neighbors. Similar to many on the spectrum who ultimately succeed, Yosef is not – perhaps cannot be – "cured" of his deficits or his disabilities. Instead, under Pharaoh's supervision, Yosef has learned to regulate his condition, to channel his talents and manage his deficits, in a manner that will produce positive results for both himself and those around him.

Conversely, though, upon further reflection, Yosef's choice to name his first son Menashe (Manasseh) – recalling the suffering he endured in his father's house[72] – may reveal a less optimistic side of Yosef's development, suggesting that rather than putting the pain of the past behind him, Yosef has held onto the memories of his difficult childhood. As explored in *HaK'sav V'haKabbala*, on its face, Yosef's recollection of his tumultuous upbringing strikes a distinctly discordant note, both implicitly, toward his brothers, and expressly – surprisingly – toward his father.[73] Although it may be possible to offer more positive interpretations,[74] a straightforward reading indicates that in fact,

71. 41:54–57.
72. 41:51.
73. See *HaK'sav V'haKabbala* 41:51.
74. See *HaK'sav V'haKabbala* 41:51.

Yosef has not gotten over the hardships he underwent at the hands of his brothers and – albeit unintentionally – his father.

At most, Yosef may have a desire to forget the pain of his childhood and to bask in his current position of power and prestige, but his words betray his inability to do so.[75] Despite his newfound success, Yosef seems to retain a substantial measure of bitterness toward his experiences with his brothers and his father, coupled with a relentless commitment to bring about the actualization of his dreams and ambitions of ruling over them, on his own terms.[76] If so, like many on the spectrum, Yosef obsesses over the insults and abuse that were inflicted upon him, unable to let go of the past – even the distant and seemingly irrelevant past, compulsively determined not only to succeed, but to remedy, repair, and replace the past, on the basis of his as-of-yet unfulfilled visions.[77]

75. Cf. Abravanel.

76. Moreover, according *Meshech Chochma*, Yosef did not share with others his reason for naming Menashe, see *Meshech Chochma* 41:51, perhaps indicating a further degree of Yosef's self-absorption and perseveration in connection with his past experiences and his remedial plans for the future.

77. Cf. *HaK'sav V'haKabbala* 41:51.

Chapter 9

Yosef and His Brothers' First Visit

INDEED, YOSEF'S BROTHERS QUICKLY re-enter the picture,[1] with the focus of the narrative suddenly shifting away from Yosef's role as Pharaoh's viceroy, returning to the personal interactions between Yosef and his family. According to a number of commentators, Yosef places himself in the position of "supplier [of food] for all of the people"[2] specifically for the purpose of insuring that he will come back into contact with his brothers.[3] Yosef anticipates that his brothers will travel to Egypt to acquire food during the years of famine, and given his role as dispenser of food supplies, they will have no option but to appear before him. Thus, far from forgetting his past, Yosef utilizes his authority primarily as a means of engineering a scenario through which he will inevitably be reunited with his brothers. However, in place of a happy reunion, Yosef devises and carries out a scheme that, yet again, seems to defy explanation.

As Yosef has expected, when Yaakov hears that there is food in Egypt, he sends ten of his sons to purchase grain.[4] When they arrive in Egypt, the brothers bow before Yosef.[5] As the text relates, Yosef recognizes his brothers, but he appears to them as an unfamiliar stranger.[6] Yosef speaks to them in a harsh manner, asking where they are from, to which they reply that they are

1. 42:1–4.
2. 42:5.
3. See Radak 42:5; Chizkuni 42:5; Abravanel.
4. 42:1–2.
5. 42:5.
6. 42:7.

from the Land of Canaan and would like to purchase food.[7] The text then states that Yosef recognizes his brothers but they do not recognize him.[8] Next, Yosef remembers his dreams about his brothers, and he begins an inquisition, starting with the immediate accusation that they are spies and culminating, after an extended dialogue, with Yosef's taking Shimon (Simeon) captive and ordering the others to go home and return with their younger brother.[9]

Commentators are puzzled by many elements of this episode. As a threshold matter, it is not clear in what manner Yosef appears – or why Yosef makes himself appear – as a stranger to his brothers. Some suggest that Yosef seems unfamiliar because in the intervening years, he has grown a beard.[10] However, others find it doubtful that such cosmetic changes would render Yosef unrecognizable to his brothers.[11] A close look at the language, dialogue, and chronology in the verses might offer a somewhat different understanding of both the nature and manner of Yosef's disguise, as well as the broader course of these events.

> And Yosef saw his brothers and he recognized them, but he made himself a stranger to them, and he spoke to them harshly, and he said to them, "From where do you come?" And they said, "From the Land of Canaan to purchase food." And Yosef recognized his brothers, and they did not recognize him. And Yosef remembered the dreams he had dreamt for them, and he said to them, "You are spies. . . ."[12]

7. 42:7.
8. 42:8.
9. 42:9–42:24.
10. See Rashi 42:8; Rashbam 42:8; Chizkuni 42:8.
11. See Radak 42:7; Ramban 42:8. In their view, Yosef's brothers simply cannot fathom that the powerful man sitting before them was once the child they had sold into slavery. See Radak 42:7; Ramban 42:8. In fact, the brothers may believe that Yosef had been killed after they sold him. See Radak 42:22; Ramban 42:22.
12. 42:7–9. The translation – "for them" – which is consistent with the interpretations of Radak and Abravanel, among others, is based on the verse's use of the word *la'hem* instead of *alehem*. Nevertheless, other commentators – including Rashi – understand the word *la'hem*, in this context, to have the same meaning as *alehem*, translated as "about them."

The text seems to indicate that the primary reason the brothers are initially unable to recognize Yosef is that, upon first seeing them, Yosef disguises himself. The text uses the reflexive form of the verb, *va'yitnaker* ("he made himself a stranger"),[13] implying that Yosef actively causes himself to appear as a stranger to them.[14] Yosef then immediately speaks to his brothers in a harsh manner,[15] which some commentators understand as a particularly effective means of hiding his true identity from them.[16]

Still, the chronology of the subsequent verses seems anomalous. After recounting Yosef's initial inquiry to his brothers about where they are from,[17] followed by their response that they are from Canaan and want to buy food,[18] the text then reports – or repeats – that Yosef recognizes his brothers and they do not recognize him.[19] At this point, Yosef remembers his dreams, after which he accuses the brothers of being spies.[20]

A possible explanation for the chronology of these verses may begin with a more complete consideration of the word *va'yitnaker,* which introduces Yosef's behavior toward his brothers.[21] Perhaps the reflexive tense of the word suggests not only that Yosef is disguising himself from his brothers, but that Yosef is disguising himself from his former self as well, fully embracing the role that Pharaoh has helped facilitate for him. More important than any changes in Yosef's appearance, Yosef adopts the persona of a mature individual who speaks harshly to others with an air that exudes confidence and authority, a manner of speaking that his brothers do not associate with the socially awkward *na'ar* they recall from their youth.[22]

---

13. 42:7.
14. See Radak 42:7; Ramban 42:7; Abravanel.
15. 42:7.
16. See Radak 42:7; Abravanel; Malbim 42:7, 8.
17. 42:7.
18. 42:7.
19. 42:8. See *Meleches Machsheves* 42:8.
20. 42:9.
21. 42:7.
22. It is not uncommon for individuals on the spectrum to enjoy and succeed in role-playing exercises and more formal acting. Likewise, Yosef is playing a role, which he is able to perfect under these artificial and

Taking on this role, Yosef inquires, curtly and imposingly: "From where do you come?"[23] Now it is the brothers who speak awkwardly, telling him: "From the Land of Canaan to purchase food."[24] Notably, the brothers' answer to Yosef is not responsive to his question.[25] Though Yosef ostensibly asks them simply about their land of origin, they inform him not only that they are from Canaan, but also that they have come to buy food. According to many commentators, because the brothers provide him too much information, Yosef has a basis upon which to make an otherwise unfounded accusation that they are spies.[26] As *Beis Halevi* explains, their over-informative answer is an indication that they are nervous and off-balance, feeling a need to explain their presence in Egypt.[27] Taking this analysis one step further, *Beis Halevi* suggests that Yosef specifically designed the wording of his question with the intent of prompting a tentative and tenuous response.[28] Yosef has put them on the defensive, and their apparent need to protest only confirms that they have something to hide.

In fact, Yosef has succeeded in effecting a role reversal,

---

stylized conditions. Therefore, it is not at all surprising that the brothers do not recognize him.

Still, Yosef's ability to take on this persona does not nullify his social deficits in other settings. Rather, Yosef has been provided supports and protections in other areas of his life, leaving him to shine in his position of power and authority, where he can exercise his unparalleled economic wisdom and administer his brilliant plan that has saved both Egypt and the surrounding lands. Within this context, empowered by the confidence that accompanies his success, Yosef can begin to take control of his social interactions as well.

23. 42:7.

24. 42:7.

25. See *HaK'sav V'haKabbala* 42:9; *Beis Halevi* 42:9.

26. See *Beis Halevi* 42:9 (describing this explanation as "well-known"). See also *HaK'sav V'haKabbala* 42:9; Malbim 42:7.

27. See *Beis Halevi* 42:9.

28. Specifically, because Yosef uses the phrase "from where are you coming," 42:7, rather than "from where are you," his brothers think he might also be asking why they came to Egypt. When their answer includes information about the reason for their visit as well, Yosef takes the opportunity to accuse them of saying too much because they are trying to conceal that they are spies. See *Beis Halevi* 42:9. Cf. Malbim 42:7.

placing his brothers in the same awkward and insecure position that he repeatedly occupied in the past. Now it is they who are unable to navigate their social interactions, unsure how to respond to others and, as a result, saying too much and saying the wrong thing. As commentators explain in further detail, the ensuing conversation between Yosef and his brothers continues to proceed in this manner.[29] Yosef skillfully and methodically levels additional accusations, each time eliciting from his brothers awkward responses that include seemingly extraneous information.[30] Ultimately, through the course of the conversation, Yosef succeeds in manufacturing a scenario in which the brothers will feel compelled to prove their innocence by leaving one of their own with him in Egypt and committing to return with their younger brother.[31]

In reality, throughout their conversation, all of the brothers' answers to Yosef are truthful. If anything, from their perspective, their responses should have demonstrated their candor and sincerity and should have worked to exonerate them from further suspicion.[32] Yosef, however, having been on the other side of this kind of social encounter, now plays the role of the cunning inquisitor and turns the brothers' responses on their head, using their own words against them, to their detriment.

A more troubling and basic question remains as to why Yosef chooses to deceive his brothers, to the point of nearly tormenting them, particularly in a way that causes further pain to his father as well. This question has puzzled generations of commentators,[33] who offer a wide variety of answers, broadly premised on the notion that Yosef wants to make sure his dreams come true,[34] and in so doing, he treats his brothers commensu-

29. See Abravanel; *Beis Halevi* 42:9.

30. See *Beis Halevi* 42:9.

31. 42:15–24.

32. See Abravanel; *Beis Halevi* 42:9.

33. Indeed, the puzzling nature of Yosef's conduct prompted at least one midrashic suggestion that Yosef initially intended to act kindly toward his brothers, but an angel appeared and told him that they were going to kill him. See *Torah Shelema* 42:7 [43].

34. See *Torah Shelema* [50] and note [50]; Ramban 42:9; Abravanel 42:7: *HaK'sav V'HaKabbala* 41:51, 42:9, 44:1, 45:1; *Michtav M'Eliyahu*

rate with the way they treated him.[35] Building on this premise, another close look at the chronology of the verses may provide a deeper understanding of Yosef's personality and his actions.

When Yosef initially sees his brothers, he has reason to believe that his dreams have already come to fruition. He has achieved greatness, and now his brothers have bowed before him for the purpose of obtaining food,[36] seeming to confirm key elements of his dreams.[37] Maybe, however, these events are insufficient to satisfy Yosef. He needs his brothers to demonstrate that they recognize who he has become, and to acknowledge for themselves the extent to which he has transformed from the immature *na'ar* they had hated, belittled, and sold, removing him from their midst.

Thus, Yosef decides to test his brothers' willingness and ability to accept his transformation, disguising himself by speaking in a way that reflects the success he has achieved.[38] Using a harsh and cunning tone, Yosef poses the intentionally ambiguous question, "From where are you coming?"[39] The brothers' awkward and potentially self-incriminatory response, "From the Land of Canaan to purchase food,"[40] has essentially sealed their own fate, as they have provided Yosef with the ammunition to accuse them of being spies.[41] They have fallen right into his trap. Accordingly, the verse now states – for the first time – that the brothers do not recognize Yosef.[42] They would never imagine Yosef, the socially inept dreamer, to be so calculating and so clever, so focused and precise in his discourse that he

---

2:236–37. See also Nechama Leibowitz, *Studies in Bereishis* (Hebrew) 325–28.

35. See Abravanel 42:15 ("All of Yosef's actions were to punish them for their sins as befitting them, *midah k'neged midah* [measure for measure]."). See Abravanel, at length: 43:15, 44:18. See also *Torah Shelema* note [46]; Rashbam 42:28; Sforno 42:28; Chizkuni 42:28; *HaK'sav V'haKabbala* 42:28, 45:1.

36. 42:6.

37. 37:7. See *Torah Shelema* [41], [49]; Rashi 42:9; Abravanel.

38. Cf. Radak 42:7; Abravanel.

39. 42:7. See *Beis Halevi* 42:9. See also Abravanel.

40. 42:7.

41. See *HaK'sav V'haKabbala* 42:9; *Beis Halevi* 42:9.

42. 42:8.

can place them on the defensive and lead them to stumble so badly in their response.

Likewise, the verse repeats that Yosef recognizes his brothers,[43] perhaps implying that he recognizes their character – that unlike Yosef, they have not been transformed over the years. Instead, they remain the same as they had been, still unable to appreciate Yosef's skills and talents. At this point, Yosef fully remembers the dreams that he dreamt "for them,"[44] recalling that his dreams related not only to himself but were also directed to his brothers, who were expected to react with respect and admiration for the success he would achieve.[45] Yosef also remembers, however, that when he told his brothers of his dreams, they instead responded by mocking him, viewing him as but a wistful and immature *na'ar* and his ambitions as the unattainable whims of a dreamer.[46] Now, he realizes, they continue to picture him in the same way. Therefore, Yosef decides that he will demonstrate the full extent of his transformation, by dominating the conversation to elicit further admissions and concessions from them.[47]

Whatever the underlying motive, Yosef is clearly determined to make sure his dreams come true, to his own satisfaction, and he continues to manufacture a series of elaborate events that will culminate in the recognition by both the brothers and Yaakov that Yosef's ambitions were correct all along. The intricate degree to which Yosef devises and engineers his scheme, closely supervising every step of the process and anticipating each turn of events, is consistent with the obsessive personality of individuals on the spectrum who, at times, despite their deficits in other areas, may perseverate on and persevere in achieving the dreams and goals that are at the center of their world. To be sure, Yosef shows some sensitivity to the feelings of others; for example, out of mercy for his brother, he will later

43. 42:8.

44. 42:9.

45. See Radak 42:9; Abravanel; *HaK'sav V'haKabbala* 42:9. See also Ramban 42:9; Sforno 42:9.

46. See Radak 42:9; Abravanel.

47. 42:9–24.

excuse himself to a private room and cry.[48] Still, Yosef largely adheres to his self-absorbed focus on his own perspective, stubbornly and inflexibly sticking to his brilliant – if somewhat outlandish – plans.

Meanwhile, Yosef's brothers slowly begin to undergo a transformation of their own. When Yosef tells the brothers that he will hold one of them captive and he orders the rest to return with their younger brother,[49] they finally express, amongst themselves, regret for what they did to Yosef.[50] In the course of their conversation, the brothers describe in detail the extent of the cruelty they exhibited toward Yosef,[51] including their belief that they caused his death.[52]

Notably, the brothers engage in this open and detailed confession in the presence of Yosef, who overhears them.[53] Although they apparently have reason to believe that Yosef does not understand Hebrew, as he has been speaking with them through an interpreter,[54] it would be prudent for them to consider that others might have the ability to hear them[55] and to understand them.[56] Indeed, the text may imply that the interpreter, who

---

48. 43:30.

49. 42:16, 19–20.

50. See 42:21–22; Nechama Leibowitz, *Studies in Bereishis* (Hebrew) 329–33.

51. 42:21–22.

52. See Radak 42:22; Ramban 42:22.

53. 42:23.

54. 42:23.

55. It seems clear that there are others present with them, in contrast to a later encounter, during which Yosef specifically orders everyone else to be removed from before him, thereby leaving him alone with his brothers. 45:1.

56. According to Ramban, 45:12–13, many Egyptians were fluent in Hebrew, and thus it should occur to the brothers that among those nearby, someone might overhear them, understand them, and inform Yosef. Alternatively, the brothers should be concerned that, despite the presence of an interpreter, the Egyptian ruler knows enough Hebrew to understand what they are saying. According to *Beis Halevi,* when Yehudah later equates Yosef with Pharaoh, he is invoking Yosef's presumed ability – like Pharaoh – to understand Hebrew. See *Beis Halevi* 44:18. In any event, at some point the brothers seem to conclude that Yosef speaks Hebrew, such that when Yehudah later speaks to Yosef, it is presumably in Hebrew

certainly understands Hebrew, is likewise present and overhears their conversation.[57] Thus, the brothers display an additional degree of recklessness and a failure to navigate their surroundings, speaking in a way that may bring great danger upon themselves.

The brothers experience a further sense of confusion – and accordingly, remorse – when they begin their return journey to Canaan and find that Yosef has placed their money back in their bags, along with the food they purchased and provisions for their trip.[58] Yosef again succeeds in throwing them off-balance, causing them to fear that they will be defenseless against false accusations of having stolen the money.[59] Significantly, they attribute their latest misfortune to God,[60] a further indication that they acknowledge and regret what they did to Yosef, and they recognize their current situation as a form of Divine punishment.

Yosef's brothers then return to Yaakov and report on the events in Egypt.[61] Strikingly, their manner of speaking now echoes the rambling manner of Yosef's earlier monologues, as they recount in detail their conversation with Yosef, without allowing Yaakov to absorb all that has occurred since he last saw them.[62] They are clearly flustered and embarrassed by their experience, and they have trouble processing and understanding the way their encounter with Yosef has turned out. *HaK'sav V'haKabbala* notes their depiction of their conversation with Yosef as *korot* (happenings),[63] connoting strange, sudden, and unexpected events.[64] As a result of their confusion and insecurity, while apparently attempting an explanation,[65] the brothers

and apparently without the assistance of an interpreter. See 44:18; *Torah Shelema* [65]; Abravanel; *Beis Halevi* 44:18.

57. 42:23.

58. 42:25, 27–28.

59. See Rashi 42:28; Sforno 42:28. See also Radak 42:35.

60. 42:28.

61. 42:29.

62. 42:30–34.

63. 42:29.

64. See *HaK'sav V'haKabbala* 42:29.

65. Ramban suggests that the brothers modified some of the details of their conversation with Yosef, in a desperate attempt to mollify Yaakov.

essentially confess their own culpability, admitting to Yaakov that their own actions were largely the cause of their present predicament. They concede to Yaakov that in their defense against Yosef's accusations, they volunteered that they had another brother at home, which in turn prompted Yosef's order that they bring their younger brother back with them.[66]

When Yaakov – unsurprisingly – refuses to allow them to take Binyamin to Egypt,[67] Reuven tries to convince him to reconsider his decision.[68] If the brothers' initial report to Yaakov is somewhat awkward, Reuven's plea to Yaakov is downright bizarre, premised on the promise that "you can kill my two sons if I do not bring [Binyamin] to you."[69] A number of *midrashim* and commentators note the absurdity of Reuven's remark,[70] to the extent that one midrash characterizes Reuven's statement as a paradigm of nonsense.[71] Indeed, in another indication of the role reversal that Yosef has engineered, now the midrash refers to Reuven as the *shoteh*.[72]

Yaakov's reaction is telling, as he does not merely reject Reuven's plea, but deems it unworthy of response.[73] Rather than dignifying Reuven's remark with an answer, Yaakov turns to his children and declares that "my son will not go with you."[74] Of course, Reuven undoubtedly intended to demonstrate to Yaakov the degree of his commitment to return from Egypt with Binyamin, but his words betray him. The brothers again find themselves so disoriented as a result of their experience with Yosef that they are unable to navigate their situation and articulate their thoughts in a way that makes sense to others.

When time passes and their provisions run out, Yaakov tells

See Ramban 42:34.

66. 42:31–34.

67. 42:36.

68. 42:37.

69. 42:37.

70. See *Torah Shelema* [102], [103], [104]; Rashi 42:38; Radak 42:37; Abravanel.

71. See *Torah Shelema* [104].

72. See *Torah Shelema* [103] and note [103].

73. See *Torah Shelema* [102]; Radak 42:37; Abravanel.

74. 42:38.

his sons to go purchase food,[75] but Yehudah reminds him of Yosef's warning not to return without their other brother.[76] For his part, Yaakov remains upset at their ineptitude and asks why they had volunteered information about Binyamin.[77] At this point, the brothers are at such a loss, and their errors have become so embarrassingly obvious, that they apparently try to escape blame by evasively telling Yaakov that Yosef initially inquired whether they had another brother.[78] Although Yaakov does not respond, Yehudah speaks up again and skillfully persuades Yaakov, who sends the brothers back to Egypt, along with gifts, the money they had found in their bags, additional money, and Binyamin.[79]

75. 43:2.

76. 43:3–5.

77. 43:6. See Abravanel.

78. 43:7. See Ramban 42:34; Abravanel. But see *Torah Shelema* 43:7 [6] (quoting the midrashic view that Yosef did initially ask them about another brother).

79. 43:8–14.

Chapter 10

Yosef and His Brothers' Second Visit

WHEN HIS BROTHERS ARRIVE in Egypt for the second time, Yosef sees that they have brought Binyamin with them, and having apparently devised the next stage of his plan, Yosef arranges to have them taken to his house to eat with him.[1] Meanwhile, the brothers remain off-balance and on the defensive, self-conscious about the past and apprehensive about the future. Repeating the pattern that has characterized their experiences since they first stood before Yosef in Egypt, the brothers find themselves unable to navigate their social settings and interactions, and they continue to respond with awkward behavior.

Without any suggestion that they are going to be punished, the brothers speculate that they are being brought to Yosef's house to be harmed and enslaved as a consequence of having had the money in their bags after their previous visit.[2] Moreover, without any prompting, the brothers approach the man who is in charge of Yosef's house and they once again incriminate themselves, offering a rambling narrative of finding money in their bags, accompanied by the insistence that they did not know who put the money there.[3] In addition to volunteering potentially inculpatory information about having left Egypt in possession of money that did not belong to them, the brothers seem to protest too much. They declare that they are prepared to return the money that they found, and they

1. 43:15–17.
2. 43:18.
3. 43:19–22.

add an unsolicited denial of any culpability on their part.[4] Of course their words are true, but their defensive protestations seem unnecessary, raising the specter that they may need to cover up a guilty conscience.

In fact, there is no indication that anyone in Egypt had paid close enough attention to know, or even notice, that among the myriad of visitors, they had left with extra money in their bags – let alone that anyone in Egypt now remembers this incident, which has long since passed, or has any desire to punish them. Even if Yosef somehow knows about the money, which apparently amounted, at most, to the sum that the brothers had brought to purchase food on their first visit, surely as viceroy, who is deciding the fate of all of the Egyptians and the visitors from the surrounding lands, he has more important priorities. It is now the brothers who are so self-absorbed in their own experiences and concerns that they make ungrounded assumptions and self-detrimental statements, without considering the scenario from the perspectives of others.

Notably, the brothers' encounter with Yosef's assistant transpires in a public setting, outside the entrance to Yosef's house.[5] According to Rashi, during the course of the conversation the man tries to push the brothers into the house, but they resist, because they fear the fate that they think awaits them inside.[6] Ironically, the midrash suggests that Yosef's motivation for bringing them into his house is not to find a venue for punishment, but rather to avoid causing them public embarrassment.[7] Instead, due to their unnecessary fears, which are the result of their unfounded conjectures, the brothers create a public altercation with Yosef's assistant, during which they volunteer an awkward public confession about a long past incident, likely

4. 43:21–22.

5. 43:19.

6. See Rashi 43:24; *Torah Shelema* [52] and note [52]. In addition, maybe out of fear or because they are flustered, their description of where they opened their bags and found the money is not entirely accurate. See 43:21; Abravanel. See also *Torah Shelema* [54]; *HaK'sav V'haKabbala* 43:21.

7. See *Torah Shelema* [48].

forgotten, forgiven, or altogether unnoticed, which has become the subject of their obsessions.

When the brothers finish their rambling protest, the man tells them not to fear because God has given them a present, he brings Shimon out to them, and he escorts them into Yosef's house.[8] The man's response not only begins to dispel their concerns, but more importantly, it shows them just how badly they have misread the situation. First, the man's reference to God mirrors their own assumption that the money in their bags was a Divine punishment,[9] but in a stunning reversal, they now learn that, to the contrary, it was a gift from God. Second, instead of taking them captive, the man brings Shimon out of captivity. Finally, in contrast to the danger they feared would confront them, when the man brings them inside Yosef's house, he provides water for them to wash and provisions for their camels, and preparations are underway for them to have a meal with Yosef.[10]

This episode represents yet another important turn of events in the brothers' continuing transformation. The stark difference between their fearful expectations and the generous welcome that actually awaited them demonstrates to the brothers that they are really the dreamers, who are unable to recognize the reality that surrounds them. They constructed an elaborate image of their future fortunes, leading them to act rashly and recklessly, only to find that the assumptions they made with great certainty were all sorely mistaken and misguided. Having already acknowledged the wrongfulness of what they did to Yosef, maybe they will now take their newfound introspection one step further and begin to reconsider their assessment of Yosef as the dreamer who will never attain any success. If they can be so wrong about their understanding of their own reality, maybe they should rethink their understanding of Yosef's reality as well.

Perhaps just as strikingly and just as significantly, this entire course of events has been orchestrated by Yosef himself,

8. 43:23.
9. 42:28.
10. 43:24–25.

through careful and clever planning and close attention to detail. As his success continues to unfold along the lines of his dreams and ambitions, Yosef continues to undergo his own profound transformation, developing an increasing willingness to consider and appreciate the perspectives of others, manifested in his ability to anticipate, with great skill and precision, each stage of his brothers' thought process and to formulate effective responses to achieve the ends he has envisioned for himself and for them.

When Yosef walks into the house, the brothers immediately bow to him,[11] and when he asks about their father, they bow yet again.[12] *Midrashim* enumerate three times the brothers have now bowed before Yosef,[13] corresponding to his two dreams[14] and to their mocking challenge to him when they asked, "Will you be king over us?"[15] The midrash seems to suggest that the brothers, having been transformed by their experiences, are ready to begin to accept Yosef's dreams. Although they still do not realize this is Yosef, the brothers have gradually developed a willingness to acknowledge the errors of many of their past assumptions; likewise, they will soon be willing to admit that they erred in their assumptions about Yosef and their rejection of his dreams, which at this point have almost all come true.

For now, however, Yosef is not finished with his brothers, and he persists in keeping them off-balance. When he sits to eat with them, Yosef engages in conduct that puzzles them.[16] He then devises a plan to fill the brothers' bags with food and money and have his goblet placed in Binyamin's bag.[17] Finally,

11. 43:26.
12. 43:28.
13. See also 42:6.
14. See *Torah Shelema* [66].
15. See 37:8; *Torah Shelema* [72].
16. 43:33. Commentators offer various suggestions as to what the brothers find surprising in Yosef's conduct. See *Torah Shelema* [96] and note [96]; Rashbam 43:33; Radak 43:33; Chizkuni 43:33.
17. 44:1–2. According to *Meshech Chochma*, when Yosef drinks wine with the brothers, 43:34, he is likewise carrying out a part of his elaborate plan. Specifically, Yosef anticipates a possible objection that may later be raised to the seemingly anomalous apprehension of Binyamin – an alleged thief – to become a servant in his house. Yosef preempts

when the brothers begin their journey back to Canaan, Yosef sends his assistant after them and tells him the precise method he should use to apprehend them[18] and the exact words he should use to accuse them of taking the goblet.[19]

When they are confronted by Yosef's assistant, the brothers continue to respond awkwardly and to their own self-detriment. In attempting to defend themselves against the assistant's accusations, they repeat their claim that they returned the money they had found in their bags after their first visit, and on that basis, they ask rhetorically how they can be suspected of stealing gold or silver from Yosef's house.[20] Again, although these statements are both true, they do not seem to help the brothers' case.

The brothers' argument is premised on their version of an episode of somewhat dubious origin, which may be seen to incriminate them just as much as – if not more than – it may exonerate them. As far as the brothers know, Yosef's assistant may reject their premise and conclude that they had, in fact, stolen the money during their first visit, then returned it solely because they were afraid to be caught, and now they are trying to steal again. Alternatively, he may now suspect that they had initially manufactured a situation in which they would appear to voluntarily return money they were mistakenly given, so that they would be able to claim innocence if they were later caught carrying out an actual act of theft. Of course, in reality they did not steal anything, on either occasion, but in relying on the expectation that Yosef's assistant will simply accept their straightforward version of the truth, the brothers fail to consider his perspective and appreciate the possibility that their claims might appear less than credible in the eyes of others.

In fact, the brothers do not stop there. They proceed to ramble on, boldly and brashly proposing that whoever stole the

---

any such objection by drinking wine with his brothers until they become intoxicated, so that he can later attribute the alleged theft to Binyamin's drunkenness, ostensibly mitigating the likelihood of a repeat offense. See *Meshech Chochma* 43:34.

18. 44:4. See Abravanel in detail; *HaK'sav V'haKabbala* 44:4.
19. 44:4–5. See Abravanel; *HaK'sav V'haKabbala* 44:5.
20. 44:7–8.

goblet should be killed and the rest should be taken as slaves.[21] The undue harshness of their rash suggestion is so apparent that the man replies that only the one who took the goblet will be enslaved, and the others will go free.[22] The brothers intend their overstated suggestion as a way of bolstering their self-assured claim of innocence, but they soon find out yet again that their perception of reality is incorrect, that as it turns out, to their utter surprise, the goblet is discovered in Binyamin's sack.[23]

The brothers are now ready to continue along the paths of both true repentance and personal transformation, corresponding directly to sins they committed in their mistreatment of Yosef.[24] First, they rend their garments,[25] which, as the midrash observes,[26] parallels having caused Yaakov to rend his garments when they told him Yosef had been killed.[27] Second, when they return to Yosef's house, they again fall before him, which the midrash correlates with Yosef's second dream,[28] of the sun and the moon bowing to him.[29] Thus, the brothers unwittingly – perhaps subconsciously – play a further role in bringing Yosef's dreams to fruition.

For his part, Yosef has remained in his house[30] awaiting their return,[31] so that he can facilitate the completion of their repentant transformation.[32] Yosef speaks to them tersely, asking, rhetorically, what they have done, and did they not perceive his stature and depth of knowledge.[33] Commentators differ as to whether Yosef is describing himself as a leader who has a deep

21. 44:9.
22. 44:10.
23. 44:12.
24. See Abravanel.
25. 44:13.
26. See *Torah Shelema* [28].
27. 37:34.
28. See *Torah Shelema* [33].
29. 37:9.
30. 44:14.
31. See Rashi 44:14.
32. See Abravanel ("so that they will be in Yosef's eyes *ba'aley teshuva g'murim* [fully repentant]").
33. 44:15.

sense of wisdom and awareness of the events around him,[34] or as a sorcerer possessing magical powers that provide him information.[35] Either way, the brothers realize that, be it by virtue of his superior wisdom or through the skillful use of magic, Yosef has outmatched them. Yosef has prevailed in the extended and one-sided battle of wits that he so carefully orchestrated, and the brothers will now have to concede defeat.

Accordingly, Yehudah's response to Yosef is one of abject surrender, an admission that there is nothing they can say to this leader, no words to speak, no way to be exonerated, as God has discovered – or uncovered – their sin.[36] The midrash understands Yehudah's tripartite admission as a three-pronged confession of guilt, corresponding to the money from the brothers' first visit, the money from their second visit, and the goblet.[37] Although Yehudah knows that they sincerely returned the money they had found in their possession after their first visit and they did not steal any money on their second visit, and he surely believes that Binyamin did not steal the goblet, at this point, they have given up all hope. Any further protestations would prove futile, as God has decided their guilt. Indeed, some commentators understand Yehudah's statement as a categorical – if implicit – denial of Yosef's accusations, accompanied by a concession that it will nevertheless be impossible for the brothers to demonstrate their innocence, because God has adjudicated them guilty for their earlier sin.[38]

The brothers once and for all recognize that they are subject to forces, both human and Divine, beyond their control, that the

---

34. See Saadia Gaon 44:15; Rashi 44:15.

35. See Abravanel.

36. 44:16.

37. See *Torah Shelema* [36]; Rabbenu Chananel 44:16; Chizkuni 44:16; *Mei Hashiloach* 44:16.

38. See *Torah Shelema* [36]; Rabbenu Chananel 44:16; Sforno 44:16; Abravanel. Therefore, Rabbenu Chananel and Abravanel explain, Yehudah refers to Binyamin as "the man in whose hand the goblet is found," 44:16, in an effort to avoid ascribing any guilt to him. See also Talmud Bavli, Shabbat 105a (reading Yehudah's words as an acronym for an implicit declaration of their innocence). But see *Torah Shelema* [26], [27], and note [26] (quoting the view in some *midrashim* that, at least initially, the brothers believed the accusations against Binyamin).

truth as they know it is sometimes contradicted by the reality of the world around them, that they feel as if they are living in a dream and are having trouble navigating their surroundings and anticipating what the future will bring. At the same time, Yehudah implicitly acknowledges their sinful behavior toward Yosef as the underlying cause of their current predicament,[39] expecting that just as they sold Yosef into slavery, the brothers will now face their own future as slaves.[40] The brothers have finally accepted full responsibility for their actions, and, as an expression of true repentance, they are prepared to accept punishment commensurate with their culpability.[41]

Yosef, however, seems to have one last task for them, responding that only the one who has the goblet – i.e., Binyamin – will be taken as a slave, while the rest will return in peace to their father.[42] If Yosef's response is intended as a test, Yehudah accepts and lives up to the challenge, forcefully and painstakingly petitioning Yosef to take him in place of Binyamin. In the course of this final showdown, both Yosef and his brothers proceed in ways that further illustrate the transformations they have respectively undergone.

In describing Yehudah's reaction to Yosef, the text introduces Yehudah's words with the phrase *va'yigash eylav* ("and [Yehudah] approached [Yosef]"), followed by Yehudah's request that he be permitted to speak "in the ears" of Yosef.[43] While some commentators interpret these phrases metaphorically,[44] Abravanel offers a literal portrait of Yehudah approaching and drawing near to Yosef, then speaking quietly, directly into Yosef's ears, so that his words will not be voluble to the many bystanders surrounding them.[45] As Abravanel notes, such daring conduct on the part of a commoner would constitute an affront to the

39. See Rabbenu Chananel 44:16; Sforno 44:16; Abravanel.

40. 44:16. See also Abravanel (describing the events on the basis of *midah k'neged midah*).

41. See Abravanel.

42. 44:17.

43. 44:18.

44. See *Torah Shelema* [49], [63]; Saadia Gaon 44:18; Rashi 44:18; *Mei Hashiloach* 44:18.

45. See Abravanel. See also *Kli Yakar* 44:18.

honor of the ruler of the land, accounting for Yehudah's further entreaty that Yosef not become angry at him.[46]

In fact, though, Yehudah's actions may be seen as more than merely disrespectful. Amidst a tense and bitter exchange with the viceroy of the Egyptian Empire, having been told in no uncertain terms that that his request has been denied, Yehudah physically approaches his adversary. Under these circumstances, Yehudah's actions may well have appeared, in the eyes of Yosef's guards, to constitute not only an insult but a direct threat against their ruler. As such, rather than brave and daring, Yehudah's conduct toward Yosef may be characterized as foolhardy and downright dangerous, resulting from Yehudah's lack of awareness of the way he will be perceived by others.

Similarly, one midrashic interpretation understands the term *va'yigash* to denote a willingness and preparedness on the part of Yehudah to engage in war against Yosef, should alternative methods of persuasion prove futile.[47] Whatever the merits of Yehudah's determination, the chances that he will successfully wage war against the viceroy of Egypt are so remote as to render this notion fanciful, if not foolish, suggesting that Yehudah is contemplating his actions in a way that is far removed from reality.

Likewise, Yehudah's tone – indicated by the language that he uses – implies a degree of aggressiveness and hostility that is not befitting a common foreigner who, along with countless others across the land, has relied on the viceroy of Egypt for sustenance, and who is now pleading for his brother's release. Based on midrashic readings of Yehudah's words, commentators identify thinly veiled demands, accusations, and even a threat to bring his argument before Pharaoh if Yosef remains unresponsive.[48]

---

46. See 44:18; Abravanel. According to *Gur Aryeh*, Rashi's metaphorical interpretation is premised on the recognition that it would be disrespectful for Yehudah to attempt to speak directly into the King's ear. See *Gur Aryeh* 44:18.

47. See *Torah Shelema* [48].

48. See *Torah Shelema* [64], [66], [67], [68], [71]; *Beis Halevi* 44:18; Nechama Leibowitz, *Studies in Bereishis* (Hebrew) 344–352 (citing *midrashim*).

Thus, Yehudah's behavior echoes Yosef's earlier missteps, during his first meeting with Pharaoh, which betrayed a similar failure to appreciate and abide by the social norms that regulate interactions with the King. Despite these errors in decorum, however, again echoing Yosef's dealings with Pharaoh, Yehudah is successful, beyond his expectations and imagination, ultimately convincing Yosef to reveal his true identity, and thereby achieving a measure of reconciliation among the brothers after years of distant alienation.

Still, in contrast to Pharaoh's earlier treatment of Yosef, which can be attributed to Yosef's evident brilliance outweighing his social deficits, it is not entirely clear why Yosef responds to Yehudah in such a positive way. Indeed, commentators note that Yehudah's speech to Yosef seems altogether less a petition than a mere – and verbose, if not rambling[49] – repetition of what has occurred.[50] Somehow this speech, on its face simply a capitulation to Yosef's authority and a recapitulation of their initial conversation, finally persuades Yosef to end his elaborate charade.

Part of the appeal of Yehudah's remarks undoubtedly lies in his willingness to truly take full responsibility for Binyamin, including, if necessary, to serve as a slave in his place.[51] Notably, in the course of the speech, Yehudah repeatedly refers to Binyamin as a *na'ar*,[52] possibly reflecting his self-conscious regret for the way the brothers had treated Yosef, and his subconscious attempt to atone for their earlier actions by offering to sacrifice himself for Binyamin. Yehudah's sincere desire to repent for the brothers' past sins would presumably impress and possibly have an impact on Yosef.

Perhaps, however – and perhaps as importantly – it is precisely the simple, direct – and socially awkward – nature of

49. Nechama Leibowitz notes that Yehudah's speech is the lengthiest monologue in the Book of Bereishis. See Nechama Leibowitz, *Studies in Bereishis* (Hebrew) 344. See also *Beis Halevi* 44:18 (identifying parts of the speech as seemingly extraneous and irrelevant.)

50. See Ramban 44:19; Abravanel; *Mei Hashiloach* 44:19, 44:20; *Beis Halevi* 44:18; Nechama Leibowitz, *Studies in Bereishis* (Hebrew) 344–48.

51. 44:32–34.

52. 44:22, 30–34.

Yehudah's speech that makes a positive impression on Yosef. Yehudah's straightforward yet incredulous description of the brothers' experiences stands as one more indication that the brothers now acknowledge how strange and disorienting their journey has been. They realize that they have no control over their own fate, and they have lost the ability to fathom why others have treated them in this manner, or to understand how they have arrived at their current situation.

In particular, *Beis Halevi* suggests, Yehudah is troubled and puzzled by the sequence and progression of the brothers' interactions with Yosef, from their initial dialogue, in which each of the brothers' truthful and innocent statements was met with aggressive and seemingly unprovoked, unsupported, and unrelated allegations,[53] through the subsequent events in which the brothers have been steadily confronted with increasingly hostile accusations and recriminations. As a result, Yehudah now finds himself at such a loss that he is no longer in a position to engage in debate or protest. Instead, Yehudah is left simply trying to reassure himself of the accuracy of his perceptions of reality, to the point of awkwardly asking the ruler to confirm his recollection of their conversation.[54]

Rather than being repulsed by Yehudah's inartful words and actions, Yosef may consider Yehudah's desperate honesty to be a refreshing and even gratifying development. Since at least the time of his brothers' first arrival in Egypt – likely much longer – Yosef has relived and perseverated on the feelings of isolation, marginalization, and bewilderment they had caused him to endure as a child. The dialogue and events that seem so mysterious to Yehudah were, in fact, the product of Yosef's carefully orchestrated plan, which he has carried out to perfection in both word and deed, with the aim of placing the brothers in a position to experience for themselves similar feelings of utter confusion, the inability to understand the reactions and responses of others, the failure to navigate their surroundings.

In this reading, Yehudah's speech impresses Yosef not in spite of his awkwardness but because of it. Yehudah now realizes

53. See *Beis Halevi* 44:18. See also Abravanel.

54. See *Beis Halevi* 44:18.

that his powers of persuasion, which he has used so skillfully and effectively in prior dealings with his brothers[55] and his father,[56] are no longer of any use to him. He has demonstrated a willingness to admit that his views of past events were sorely mistaken; accordingly, he is now ready to adjust and modify his current views as well, and to encounter a new future.[57] In short, the brothers' transformation is now complete. They are finally ready to recognize Yosef, on his own terms – to accept that he has achieved the dreams and ambitions that had been the source of their hatred and derision.

This understanding of Yehudah's transformation and the consequential impact of his speech on Yosef may shed further light on Yehudah's repeated reference to Binyamin as a *na'ar*,[58] culminating in his bold declaration to Yosef that he is ready to be taken "in place of the *na'ar*."[59] Perhaps Yehudah is also offering to change places with the first *na'ar*, the immature Yosef, whose awkward and unrealistic words and behaviors had incurred the mocking wrath of Yehudah and the other brothers. As such, Yehudah is acknowledging how foolish and disoriented he feels, now that he has lost control of his own words and actions – or at least the way they are perceived by others.

Abravanel suggests that Yehudah's willingness to serve as a slave constitutes the final stage of *midah k'neged midah* (measure for measure), corresponding to Yehudah's decision to sell Yosef into slavery.[60] Likewise, perhaps Yehudah's ability to identify as a *na'ar* comprises the final piece of a different kind of *midah k'neged midah*, representing the transformation he and his brothers have undergone: it is the brothers whose be-

55. See, e.g., 37:26–38.

56. See, e.g., 43:8–15.

57. Yehudah had previously undergone a somewhat similar transformation during the events involving Tamar, 38:26, which are otherwise unrelated to the narrative surrounding Yosef, and in some ways seem to interrupt the story. See 38:1–30; Rashi 38:1; Ibn Ezra 38:1; Radak 38:1. The episode of Yehudah and Tamar may thus serve as a precursor, setting the stage for Yehudah's transformative experiences in his encounters with Yosef.

58. 44:22, 30, 31, 32.

59. 44:33–34.

60. See Abravanel.

haviors now resemble those of individuals on the spectrum.[61] Accordingly, they finally find within themselves the ability to understand and to feel the way they had caused Yosef to feel.

> . . . And [Yosef] called out, "Remove all of the men from before me," and no man stood with him when Yosef made himself known to his brothers. And he gave his voice to a cry, and Egypt heard and the house of Pharaoh heard. And Yosef said to his brothers, "I am Yosef, is my father still alive?" and his brothers could not respond because they were stunned by him. And Yosef said to his brothers, "Please come close to me," and they came close, and he said, "I am Yosef your brother that you sold to Egypt. And now, do not be sad . . .

---

61. As the story proceeds, the brothers continue to exhibit other behaviors characteristic of individuals on the spectrum. For example, the text states that after Yosef discloses his identity, the brothers are unable to respond because *nivhalu mi'panav,* 45:3, which literally denotes their fear of his face. Perhaps, as is common for individuals on the spectrum, the brothers are unable to look at Yosef's face – to look him in the eye – during their tense, emotional, and now shocking interchange with him. Yosef then repeats "I am Yosef," 45:4, perhaps echoing Pharaoh's earlier statement to Yosef – "I am Pharaoh," 41:44 – which may have been necessary as a means of refocusing Yosef, who at the time was possibly lost in his own thoughts and dreams. Likewise, a midrash describes the brothers as looking about the room, such that Yosef needs to redirect them toward himself. See *Torah Shelema* 45:4 [18].

In addition, after Yosef tells the brothers his plans for their retrieval of Yaakov and their return to Egypt, he says that "your eyes and . . . Binyamin's eyes see that my mouth is speaking to you." 45:12. Yosef's emphasis on their eyes seeing his mouth – rather than, for example, their ears hearing the words of his mouth – may indicate that they avoided looking at his face.

Finally, in recalling – first to Yaakov and later to Yosef – their initial encounter and conversation with Yosef, the brothers quote Yosef as having warned them that "you will not see my face" unless they bring Binyamin to him. 43:5; 44:23. Perhaps the brothers' emphasis on their inability to see Yosef's face – a phrase that, it turns out, is not recorded as part of Yosef's statement to them – reflects their recognition that, starting from their initial meeting, they were beginning to feel and act like they were on the spectrum, unable to look Yosef in the eye. Cf. *Tzafnas Pane'ach al HaTorah* 42:8 (stating that the brothers did not recognize Yosef when they first arrived in Egypt because they did not look directly at his face).

> you did not send me here, but God, and He placed me as an adviser to Pharaoh and a master of all of his palace and a ruler in all of the Land of Egypt. Go quickly and bring my father and say to him. . . ."[62]

When Yosef decides to reveal his identity to his brothers, the manner in which he proceeds may demonstrate both the extent and the limits of the transformation he has undergone. For example, before addressing his brothers, Yosef instructs that everyone else should be removed from his presence.[63] Although several commentators and *midrashim* praise Yosef's apparent desire to protect both himself and his brothers from public embarrassment,[64] other *midrashim* note the risk Yosef took in casting out all of his guards, rendering himself vulnerable to an attack by his brothers, with whom he has just concluded a heated altercation.[65] Yosef's failure to recognize this potential danger may illustrate a reversion to a more general lack of awareness of his social setting, coupled with an inability both to understand the effect that his actions will have on others and to anticipate their reactions.

Perhaps more tellingly, Yosef's conduct may have – presumably unwittingly, but still unhelpfully – provoked a high level of apprehension in his brothers. First, to the extent that Yosef left himself open to an attack by his brothers, they, in turn, might have feared that he intended to attack them. The text introduces Yosef's instruction to clear the room with the word *va'yikra* ("and he called out"), which Ramban understands to imply that he raised his voice in anger.[66] Next, immediately after Yosef is left alone with his brothers, he cries out in a way that is audible to "Egypt" and the "house of Pharaoh."[67] The precise nature and significance of Yosef's crying out is open to interpretation,[68]

62. 45:1–5, 8–9.

63. 45:1.

64. See *Torah Shelema* 45:1 [8] and notes [7], [8]; Rashi 45:1; Ramban 45:1–2; Abravanel.

65. See *Torah Shelema* [7], [8].

66. See Ramban 45:1–2.

67. 45:2.

68. See Abravanel. Notably, at a number of points throughout the

but to the brothers, such a voluble cry – if not scream – on the part of the visibly angry viceroy may have seemed unnerving, perhaps signaling that he was now prepared to harm them. Of course, there is no indication that Yosef intends to instill – or is even aware of – this impression on their part.

Second, the manner in which Yosef delivers his remarks to his brothers contributes to their fearful response. Yosef is exceedingly direct, simply stating that "I am Yosef," and without

---

narrative, Yosef is depicted as crying. See also 43:30, 45:14, 45:15, 46:29, 50:2, 50:17. Although in many, if not all, of these instances, it is understandable for Yosef to cry in reaction to a significant event that invites an emotional response, it remains striking that the text repeatedly describes Yosef in this manner. Moreover, in each of these instances, the text does not record any statements that accompanied Yosef's crying, suggesting that he may have been emotionally overwhelmed and therefore unable to speak. It is not uncommon for individuals on the spectrum to experience a form of sensory or emotional overload that prevents them from articulating their feelings in words, resulting instead in an outburst of helpless and panicked crying or calling out.

Yosef's tendency to become overwhelmed, and therefore unable to speak, might likewise explain his apparent silence while his brothers remove his coat, grab him, and cast him into the pit. See 37:24. See also Aryeh Leib Friedman, *Sefer Va'yevk Yosef* 34 (quoting midrashic comments regarding Yosef's repeated silence throughout the course of his tribulations). Cf. *Torah Shelema* 42:21 [78]. Although the brothers later allude to their own refusal to heed his pleadings, 42:21, the nature and substance of his petition are absent from the brothers' statement and open to interpretation. One midrash portrays Yosef as crying and screaming from inside the pit, see *Torah Shelema* 37:24 note [142], perhaps corroborating the impression that he is too overwhelmed to articulate his opposition or even to register a complaint while he is in the process of being assaulted, and that even once inside the pit, he is only able to burst out in cries and screams.

On a somewhat similar note, when Potiphar's wife grabs his garment and propositions him, Yosef's actions seem to demonstrate an inability to process the events and a tendency to become overwhelmed and panicked. At the time of her advances, Yosef is not recorded as uttering any response, or offering any physical resistance. Instead, he initially seems to surrender to her use of force, and then, in a state of alarm, he leaves his garment in her hand and flees, thereby incriminating himself. 39:12. Likewise, when she later levels false accusations at him and he is taken to prison, rather than protesting his innocence, Yosef appears once again to remain silent. 39:20.

missing a beat or giving them an opportunity to absorb this incredible news, he immediately asks if his father is still alive.[69] The brothers, understandably, are stunned, embarrassed, and scared, and accordingly unable to respond.[70] Here too, there is no indication that Yosef intended to place his brothers in fear.

If anything, commentators suggest, Yosef was trying to speak to his brothers in a way that would prevent both fear and embarrassment,[71] accounting for his attempt to change the subject from his past dealings with them to the present condition of his father.[72] If this was Yosef's goal, however, he was clearly unsuccessful.[73] Apparently, in his social interactions with his

---

69. 45:3. Some commentators suggest that Yosef was not asking whether his father was still alive – after all, Yehudah had just described, at considerable length, the harm that will befall their father if the brothers return without Binyamin – but rather, Yosef was asking rhetorically how his father could still be alive after undergoing such suffering. See Sforno 45:3; *HaK'sav V'haKabbala* 45:3. See also Abravanel; *Beis Halevi* 45:3. If so, it may be notable that Yosef, who previously may have had difficulty understanding sarcasm and rhetorical questions – which require a recognition of the nuances of nonverbal cues such as tone of voice, see 37:8; 41:38 – now uses a rhetorical question to express his wonderment at his father's survival.

70. 45:3. Commentators and midrashim have identified a variety of possible reasons for the brothers' stunned silence, see *Torah Shelema* [13*], ranging from their fear that Yosef might mete out revenge, see Chizkuni 45:3; *Beis Halevi* 45:3, to their disbelief that they had been so wrong in the way they had viewed Yosef, see *Torah Shelema* [14]; *Sichos Mussar* 5732:13, to their abject shame over how unjustified they were in their actions toward both Yosef and their father, see *Beis Halevi* 45:3, to the shock they experience at being suddenly confronted with the simple truth they have denied for so many years. *Minchas Asher*, Bereishis 561–62. Whatever the precise cause, it is notable that the brothers now feel overwhelmed and, as a result, remain silent, echoing Yosef's earlier experiences of overwhelmed panic, accompanied by his repeated inability to respond to his aggressors.

71. See Rashi 45:1; Ramban 45:1; Abravanel; *Ohr Hachaim* 45:1.

72. See Abravanel.

73. In light of the brothers' response, Yosef's subsequent attempts to put them at ease would seem similarly unavailing, if not unwise. Yosef asks the brothers to draw near to him – which, based on their current perceptions, may alert them to the possibility that he will now physically harm them – and then repeats that he is Yosef, their brother, "that you sold me to Egypt." 45:4. In this context, reminding them of the sale would only

brothers, Yosef still does not possess the skills and judgment that have served him so well in his professional position – or even the skills he had used in speaking with his brothers while under the guise of *Tzafnat Pane'ach*.

Moreover, Yosef does not seem willing to give his brothers a chance to process the startling information they have just learned. Instead, appearing utterly uninterested in waiting for their response, Yosef launches into a rambling lecture that consists of his confident depiction of God's design for himself and for them,[74] followed by urgent orders that they return to Canaan

---

seem to engender further apprehension, on their part, that Yosef is now ready to take revenge on them.

74. 45:5–8. Although Yosef's attempts to console his brothers' feelings of regret and to alleviate their fears, along with his apparent willingness to forgive them, are admirable, Yosef's recounting the fulfillment of God's design for him and his destiny as a leader seems to include unnecessary – if arguably accurate – descriptions of his success, suggesting a degree of self-absorption and self-aggrandizement. See, e.g., 45:8. See also *HaK'sav V'haKabbala* 45:12 (observing that it is somewhat unbecoming of an individual of Yosef's stature to boast about his success in this way); *Torah Shelema* [37] (understanding Yosef's statements about God's plan for him as alluding to his coat of colors and his dreams). Apparently, Yosef still feels the need – all these years later, and with all of the events that have passed – to articulate to himself and prove to his brothers that he was right all along. It seems that, like some individuals on the spectrum, even after Yosef achieves success, his self-absorbed perspective induces a desire to demonstrate, both to himself and to others, that his dreams and visions have come to fruition.

Significantly, though Yosef might be satisfied – or self-satisfied – with the way the events have unfolded, it is less than clear that Yosef's account of God's plan for his own success will, in fact, alleviate the brothers' regret. As Abravanel discusses at length, God's manipulation of events, bringing about a positive outcome for Yosef and, in turn, bringing about a broader Divine plan, does not serve to absolve the brothers of their personal responsibility for their actions. See Abravanel. Cf. *Minchas Asher,* Bamidbar 438–39 (citing *Ohr Hachaim* 50:20). Nevertheless, in describing the events to his brothers, Yosef continues to view the reality of his life largely from his own self-absorbed perspective rather than with a full appreciation of the feelings of others.

Perhaps a similar understanding of Yosef's character informs the Talmudic discussion of his somewhat puzzling decision, when he gives gifts to his brothers, to give additional gifts to Binyamin. 45:22. As the Talmud notes, Yosef seems to replicate Yaakov's error of favoring one

to retrieve Yaakov, and culminating in a fully developed plan of where and how they will live when they are back in Egypt.[75]

Indeed, in some ways, from the time he reveals and reclaims his personal identity, Yosef seems to leave his professional persona and revert back to his former self, the *na'ar* who breathlessly tells others his ideas, his plans, and his visions, without waiting for them to respond or even to have a chance to absorb all that he has said, however brilliant and prescient. Like many on the spectrum, having been provided the necessary assistance and professional supports, Yosef has largely learned to manage and channel his deficits, and to focus on his strengths and abilities; in so doing, he has achieved remarkable success. It is not surprising, however, that when reunited with his brothers – outside of the presence of the Egyptians and outside of the context of his persona, Yosef returns to some of his old – and odd – behaviors.

Still, Yosef is not the same *na'ar* who was lost in his own dreams and visions. Yosef is a leader, and in this capacity he is able to look beyond himself and his own future. Within this role, he is now capable of envisioning, planning, and engineering the futures of others – both individuals and nations. In his speech to his brothers, Yosef includes an intricate and elaborate plan that takes into account his brothers' feelings, Yaakov's feelings, and the perspectives of the Egyptians, with every detail thought out and plotted, up to the precise words the brothers should use

brother over the others, which was the underlying cause of the series of events that had resulted in so much trouble and tribulation. In response to this difficulty, the Talmud suggests that Yosef gave Binyamin five sets of clothing to allude to Binyamin's descendant, Mordechai (Mordecai), who would go before the King wearing five sets of royal clothing. See Talmud Bavli, Megillah 16b. Of course, as commentators note, Yosef's conduct remains problematic, as the brothers presumably do not understand this allusion, and instead they likely resent the favoritism Yosef shows toward Binyamin. See *Torah Shelema* note [79]. Perhaps the Talmud is again illustrating that Yosef views his actions and his reality through his own self-absorbed, albeit accurate, sense of destiny – this time, the destiny of Binyamin's descendant – rather than taking into account the effects his actions will have on others.

75. 45:9–11.

when they return to Yaakov.[76] Thus, Yosef has learned to moderate and modify his own impulses and ambitions, to include a measure of appreciation, understanding, and anticipation of the perceptions, expectations, and actions of others.

76. When the brothers return to Yaakov, they tell him that Yosef is alive, but he initially does not believe them. 45:26. When the brothers then tell Yaakov "all of the words of Yosef" and he sees the wagons "that Yosef sent," Yaakov declares that Yosef is still alive. 45:27. Apparently, on some level, Yosef has a better understanding of Yaakov, and how to speak to him, than do his brothers, who have lived with their father for all of this time. Perhaps Yosef's success and social acuity in this particular interaction with his brothers and his father result from Pharaoh's direct involvement in the planning process, suggesting that Yosef was still operating, for these purposes, in his official capacity and with the helpful supports of Pharaoh. See 45:17–21. Cf. Rashi 45:27; Rashbam 45:27; Chizkuni 45:27. In any event, Yosef's own interactions with Yaakov will still be fraught with awkward behaviors and misunderstandings, as illustrated by Yosef's later attempt to intervene when Yaakov blesses Yosef's children. See 48:18.

Chapter 11

Yosef and His Family in Egypt

WHEN YAAKOV AND HIS sons arrive in Egypt, Yosef continues to excel in his professional role, demonstrating qualities of leadership as he presides skillfully over a hungry, desperate, and impatient nation.[1] As conditions take a turn for the worse and all the people of Egypt complain to Yosef out of fear that they will die, Yosef composes a complex agricultural and economic strategy that ultimately saves the nation and that the people embrace. As the years of famine intensify, Yosef develops further elements of his masterful plan, emerging out of a crisis in a way that consolidates Pharaoh's power[2] while at the same time earning Yosef and Pharaoh the admiration of a now grateful nation.[3] Notably, Yosef's accomplishments once again have a close connection to dreams; pursuant to his earlier interpretations, alongside his own dreams, he has now brought the events depicted in Pharaoh's dreams to a successful conclusion as well.

Perhaps more significantly, notwithstanding his past social deficits, Yosef likewise devises and skillfully executes a plan for his brothers' interactions with Pharaoh, displaying the ability to understand and anticipate Pharaoh's preferences and personality. Yosef describes to his family the precise details of the plan: he will first inform Pharaoh that his brothers and his father have arrived from Canaan, and that they are shepherds who own livestock and have brought all their sheep, cattle, and

1. 47:13–27.
2. 47:23–24.
3. 47:25.

possessions;[4] next, when Pharaoh calls for them and asks their vocation, the family should reply: "Your servants have been owners of livestock since our youth until now, both we and our fathers."[5] As Yosef explains, this carefully crafted script will enable his family to live in the Land of Goshen, because shepherds are abominable to the Egyptians.[6] Elaborating on Yosef's explanation, commentators note that Yosef's plan was intricately designed to prompt Pharaoh to volunteer the suggestion that Yosef's family live in Goshen, thus allowing them to accomplish the desired result of dwelling apart from Pharaoh and the rest of Egypt,[7] without appearing presumptuous, ungrateful, or disrespectful.[8]

Sure enough, Yosef sets the stage by approaching Pharaoh and introducing his family: ". . . my father and my brothers and their sheep and their cattle and all they possess have arrived from the Land of Canaan, and they are in the Land of Goshen."[9] As Yosef anticipated, Pharaoh proceeds to ask the brothers about their vocation,[10] to which they answer, as Yosef instructed, "Your servants are shepherds, both we and our fathers."[11] Yet, rather than quietly and patiently awaiting Pharaoh's response, the brothers speak again, in a way that defies Yosef's instructions and potentially imperils his meticulous design. Instead of allowing Pharaoh to initiate the proposal that they live in Goshen, the brothers anxiously and awkwardly tell Pharaoh that "we came to dwell in the land because there is nowhere for your servants' sheep to graze, because the famine is severe in the Land of Canaan," and they close with the untoward request:

4. 46:31–32.

5. 46:33–34.

6. See Radak 46:34; Rabbenu Bachya 46:32; Chizkuni 46:32.

7. See *Torah Shelema* [188]; Radak 46:34; Chizkuni 46:32; Rabbenu Bachya 46:32; Abravanel; Nechama Leibowitz, *Studies in Bereishis* (Hebrew) 366–71.

8. See Sforno 46:31; Abravanel.

9. 47:1. Abravanel suggests that Yosef's minor deviations from his scripted remarks were likewise intended to plant the seed for Pharaoh to decide, ostensibly on his own, that the family should live in Goshen.

10. 47:3.

11. 47:3.

"And now, please let your servants settle in the Land of Goshen."[12]

As Abravanel observes, in place of eliciting a gracious offer from Pharaoh that they live in Goshen, the brothers have provoked Pharaoh's suspicion and indignation, prompting him to refuse to speak to them.[13] A presumably perturbed Pharaoh turns instead to Yosef, unceremoniously informing him that "your father and brothers have come to you" and directing Yosef to settle them in Goshen.[14] Pharaoh is essentially telling Yosef, in less than cordial terms, that they are Yosef's family and, accordingly, Yosef's responsibility.[15]

Ultimately, Yosef resolves the matter in a way that achieves the goal of settling his family in Goshen, while at the same time proving consistent with the interests of Pharaoh.[16] Yosef is again successful, both in his professional capacity as adviser to Pharaoh and, strikingly, in his social interactions with Pharaoh, through his ability to understand, anticipate, and orchestrate the most effective and appropriate manner of communication. His brothers, in contrast, seem to continue to exhibit the social ineptitude they have displayed since their initial meeting with Yosef in Egypt, interacting with Pharaoh in a way that nearly worked to their detriment, but for Yosef's ability to skillfully navigate and finesse an uncomfortable situation.

Still, consistent with autism spectrum disorder, although Yosef is able to succeed professionally, in part because he can compensate for his deficits by demonstrating his undeniable intellect and achievements, even years of professional prowess do not change the underlying reality of his condition. While an individual on the spectrum has much to gain, and much to offer, when provided appropriate accommodations and supports, autism spectrum disorder – though potentially responsive to treatment – is ordinarily not susceptible to being "cured." Instead, more often than not, an individual on the spectrum faces the ongoing challenge – if not failure – of trying to gen-

---

12. 47:4.
13. See Abravanel.
14. 47:5–6.
15. See *Torah Shelema* 47:5 [9] and note [9].
16. 47:10.

eralize successful behaviors outside of the structured settings where accommodations and supports are provided.

Thus, despite Yosef's ability to excel within the stylized environment of his professional setting, Yosef reverts to awkward and off-putting behaviors when he returns to his family setting. Indeed, three additional episodes suggest that Yosef continues to face challenges in his social interactions with his family, outside of the structures and strictures of his professional persona. These final episodes illustrate once more the complexity of Yosef's condition and the effect that it has on his relationships with others.

First, when Yaakov senses that he is soon going to die, he calls for Yosef.[17] At the beginning of their encounter, Yaakov asks Yosef to swear that he will bury Yaakov outside of Egypt with Yaakov's fathers,[18] but Yosef seems to refuse to take the oath, responding tersely – if not curtly – that "I will do as you have said."[19] Yaakov again directs Yosef to take an oath to him, and this time Yosef complies.[20]

Midrashim and commentators suggest that Yosef's initial refusal was based on his reasoning that the oath was unnecessary because, regardless, he fully intended to carry out Yaakov's wishes.[21] In fact, though, *midrashim* and commentators further explain, Yaakov did not question Yosef's allegiance to him, but instead was concerned that Pharaoh would not permit Yosef to leave Egypt or to bury Yaakov outside of Egypt unless he was bound under oath.[22] Indeed, Yosef references the oath when he later asks Pharaoh to allow him to bury Yaakov in Canaan,[23] and in granting Yosef's request, Pharaoh specifically tells Yosef to "go up and bury your father, as he swore you to do."[24] Apparently, as Yaakov predicted, the oath was a necessary

17. 47:29.
18. 47:29–30.
19. 47:30.
20. 47:31.
21. See *Torah Shelema* [132] and note [132]; Rabbenu Chananel 47:30; Ramban 47:31; Abravanel.
22. See *Torah Shelema* [132] and note [132]; Ramban 47:31.
23. 50:5
24. 50:6

means toward securing Pharaoh's permission.[25] Thus, Yaakov demonstrates a recognition of the impact their actions will have on others, both anticipating Pharaoh's response to Yosef's request and preempting Pharaoh's potential opposition.

Yosef, in contrast, having returned, for the purposes of this encounter, to his familial role as Yaakov's son, no longer displays the capacity to orchestrate events through insightful reflection and skillful planning. Notably, during his years as ruler over Egypt, Yosef had quite effectively navigated his official interactions with Pharaoh, including the delicate effort to convince Pharaoh to adopt a royal policy permitting his family to live in Goshen. Now, however, functioning outside of his professional role as viceroy of Egypt, Yosef seems to lose this ability.

Next, when Yaakov prepares to bless Yosef's sons, Yosef positions the older son, Menashe, at Yaakov's right, and the younger son, Ephraim, at Yaakov's left.[26] Yaakov, however, places his right hand on the head of Ephraim and his left hand on the head of Menashe.[27] A displeased Yosef takes Yaakov's right hand, intending to remove it from Ephraim's head and to place it on Menashe's head,[28] while advising Yaakov, "Not so, my father, but he is the older, place your right hand on his head."[29] Yaakov resists, responding, "I know, my son, I know," and explaining that the younger son will grow greater than the older.[30]

A number of elements contained in this brief exchange between Yosef and Yaakov are both startling and, upon close examination, quite telling as a further reflection of Yosef's condition. For example, in both word and deed, Yosef displays a somewhat troubling overconfidence – if not outright disrespect – toward his father. Yosef's willingness to second-guess Yaakov[31] may be consistent with characteristics of an individ-

---

25. See *Torah Shelema* [132] and note [132]; Rashi 50:6; Ramban 47:31; Abravanel.

26. 48:13.

27. 48:14.

28. 48:17.

29. 48:18.

30. 48:19.

31. See Ramban 48:17.

ual on the spectrum whose self-absorbed perspective may lead him to believe that, because he excels in areas of his own expertise – often defying expectations – he is likewise correct in his evaluation of other matters as well. Although Yosef has reached undeniably remarkable heights of success and has, in many ways, surpassed Yaakov in his accomplishments, it turns out that Yaakov has a more accurate understanding of the relative strengths, and futures, of Yosef's sons. Along these lines, several *midrashim* interpret Yaakov's seemingly repetitive response to Yosef – "I know . . . I know"[32] – as a forceful remonstration through which Yaakov declares that, contrary to Yosef's doubts about his awareness or even his capacity, Yaakov is far more knowledgeable than Yosef, in these and other matters.[33]

In addition to Yosef's unfounded overconfidence in his own ability to discern the truth and his misguided lack of confidence in his father's knowledge and awareness, the manner in which Yosef expresses his objections compounds the unseemliness of his attitude. Yosef's statement, "Not so, my father,"[34] strikes a decidedly discordant note, inconsistent with the proper respect that a child should show a father, but again consistent with behaviors often associated with an individual on the spectrum. Eschewing social mores, Yosef is direct in his criticism of Yaakov, seemingly feeling no compunction about brusquely accusing Yaakov of being wrong, and abruptly – and forcibly – instructing him to place his right hand on Menashe's head. Although commentators offer alternate readings that soften the substance, and presumably the tone, of Yosef's remarks,[35] the text suggests that, in both form and substance, Yosef is speaking and acting in a socially inappropriate manner.

Furthermore, when contrasted with Yaakov's conduct in this episode, Yosef's behavior seems to betray a substantial and consequential inability to understand, appreciate, and act in conformance with social nuances. Chizkuni offers the intriguing observation that, rather than switching the positions of his

32. 48:19.
33. See *Torah Shelema* [116], [117], [117*].
34. 48:18.
35. See *Torah Shelema* note [114]; Rashbam 48:17–18; Chizkuni 48:18.

hands, Yaakov could have achieved the same effect of placing his right hand on Ephraim's head by switching the positions in which Ephraim and Menashe stood before him.[36] Expounding on the use of the term *seekel et yadav* ("arranged his hands")[37] to denote the wisdom of Yaakov's action, Chizkuni explains that Yaakov intended to proceed discreetly, in a manner that would prevent embarrassment to Menashe.[38] Yaakov concluded that switching the positions of his hands would be less conspicuous, and more sensitive to Menashe's feelings, than would instructing Ephraim and Menashe to switch the places where they were standing.

If so, Yosef's attempt to correct Yaakov was not only erroneous, as well as ineptly articulated and executed, but it also called attention to Ephraim's blessing, thereby highlighting the awkward situation that Yaakov tried to downplay. Thus, Yosef's failure to read social cues, and his insistence on taking action based on his own mistaken understanding, seem to have produced an unfortunate, embarrassing, and otherwise avoidable result.

Finally, after Yaakov's death and embalmment, which are followed by extended periods of mourning and his burial in Canaan,[39] Yosef and his brothers return toward Egypt, undergoing one last encounter and engaging in a dialogue that illuminates, and brings full circle, the nature of Yosef's condition and its effect on his personal interactions and relationships.

> And Yosef's brothers saw that their father had died, and they said: "Lest Yosef hate us and return to us all of the wrong that we did to him." And they commanded Yosef, saying: "Your father commanded before he died, saying, 'Thus say to Yosef: "Please forgive the wrong of your brothers and their sin for

---

36. See Chizkuni 48:14. See also *Pachad Yitchak*, Purim 78 (considering why Yaakov did not move his own position such that Ephraim would be at his right and Menashe at his left). But see Rabbenu Bachya 48:13 (explaining that Yaakov moved Ephraim to his right and Menashe to his left).

37. 48:14.

38. See Chizkuni 48:14.

39. 49:33–50:13.

> they did harm to you.'" And now, please forgive the wrong of the servants of the God of your father."[40]

The text recounts Yosef's brothers' remarks, expressing amongst themselves the fear that since their father has died, Yosef might take revenge against them, in retaliation for all the harm they had caused him.[41] Rashi, echoing several *midrashim*, notes that the verse prefaces the brothers' statement with the phrase "Yosef's brothers saw that their father had died,"[42] implying that although months had passed since Yaakov's death, it was only at this point that the brothers began to fear Yosef, on account of what they now "saw." Thus, as Rashi notes, the text begs the question as to what the brothers saw that aroused their fear.[43] Drawing upon one of the midrashic responses to this question, Rashi explains that during Yaakov's life, out of respect for his father, Yosef had his brothers join him for meals. After Yaakov's death, the brothers saw that Yosef no longer invited them,[44] leading them to fear that he is now planning to harm them.

Notably, as a number of *midrashim* further elaborate, Yosef chose to dine alone at this point out of good intentions,[45] and as an expression of his humility. Specifically, the *midrashim* explain, over the years, in deference to Yaakov's wishes, Yosef had sat at the head of the table when eating with his family, notwithstanding Yosef's feelings that Reuven and Yehudah deserved the honor, as the oldest son and as royalty, respectively. After Yaakov's death, Yosef, as viceroy, would presumably have continued to sit at the head of the table, but he no longer felt justified in doing so on the grounds of showing respect for Yaakov. To avoid betraying the honor he considered due to Reuven and Yehudah, Yosef chose not to eat with them, thereby avoiding the predicament altogether.[46] Yosef's brothers, who are not

40. 50:15–17.
41. 50:15.
42. 50:15.
43. See Rashi 50:15. See also *Torah Shelema* 50:15 [49], [50].
44. See Rashi 50:15. See also *Torah Shelema* [49].
45. Cf. *Gur Aryeh* 50:15 (identifying positive motivations for Yosef's conduct).
46. See *Torah Shelema* [49] and note [49].

privy to this thought process, believe that he is no longer eating with them because he is planning to harm them. Despite Yosef's good intentions and admirable inner humility, Yosef is perceived by his brothers as aloof and vindictive, sparking their fear that he will now take out his long held grievances against them.[47]

Other *midrashim* offer alternative narratives, similarly depicting Yosef as well-intentioned but unable to recognize the effect that his conduct will have on others. For example, in one midrash, as Yosef and his brothers are on their journey back to Egypt, they pass the pit where the brothers had cast him when he was a teenager, and Yosef enters the pit so that he can contemplate and appreciate the wonders God showed in saving him.[48] In another version, Yosef approaches the pit and performs the religious duty of reciting a blessing at the site where God brought about miracles in his behalf.[49] In both versions, Yosef's brothers are not aware of his intentions, and therefore they reach the fearful – and, under the circumstances, entirely reasonable – conclusion that he is recalling what they did to him and is plotting his revenge.[50]

Thus, numerous *midrashim* paint a further portrait of Yosef as a self-absorbed individual who, though well-meaning in his devotion to his brothers' honor and somewhat pious in his devotion to God, nevertheless is painfully oblivious to the way others see him. Moreover, because he is unaware of the impact his actions will have on others, Yosef brings about a result that is diametrically opposed to what he is trying to accomplish. In the course of reaching his own goals and achieving the truths they embody, Yosef imperils his interpersonal relationship with his brothers, who – instead of admiring his noble intentions – suspect him of having base and ignoble motivations. For all of the brilliance and success of his professional calculations, Yosef fails to accurately evaluate and anticipate the social consequences of his actions within the context of his personal life.

47. Cf. *Mei Hashiloach* 50:20.
48. See *Torah Shelema* note [50].
49. See *Torah Shelema* [50].
50. See *Torah Shelema* [50] and note [50].

Indeed, the midrash criticizes Yosef for failing to adhere to the dictum mandating that an individual act in a manner that is acceptable in both Divine and human perspectives.[51] Yosef may have expected that his single-minded dedication would prove acceptable in Divine perspective, but his self-absorbed behaviors appear unacceptable – socially unacceptable – in human perspective. In short, once again Yosef evokes the image of an individual on the spectrum who is committed to pursuing his own ambitions – as noble as they may be in this case – without taking into account the sensitivities and reactions of others.

Whatever the precise cause of their fears, Yosef's brothers tell him that before Yaakov died, he instructed them to ask Yosef to "forgive the wrong of your brothers and their sin for they did harm to you."[52] However, there is reason to doubt that Yaakov actually left the brothers with such an instruction.[53] In fact, the Talmud, *midrashim*, and many commentators operate under the assumption that Yaakov never gave this command to his sons,[54] and the Talmud and *midrashim* thereby derive from this episode the principle that a person may lie for the purpose of securing peace.[55] Yosef's brothers were justified in fabricating a command that they attributed to their father, to preserve the peace between themselves and Yosef.

Yet, the assumption that Yaakov did not issue this order to his children raises the question as to why Yaakov did not share

51. See *Torah Shelema* note [50]. See also Nechama Leibowitz, *Studies in Bereishis* (Hebrew) 399–402.

52. 50:16–17.

53. First, throughout the extensive narrative of the story of Yaakov and his sons, there is no other account of this instruction. See *Torah Shelema* note [54]. Second, if Yaakov did, in fact, want to convey this request to Yosef, it would seem odd to communicate the information through a message from the brothers – whose credibility and authority in this matter were, to say the least, quite compromised – rather than making the request directly to Yosef. Cf. Ramban 45:27. Finally, it is not clear that Yaakov knew the brothers had harmed Yosef. See Ramban 45:27.

54. See Talmud Bavli, Yevamot 65b; *Torah Shelema* [54] and note [54]; Rashi 50:16; Ramban 45:27. See also Nechama Leibowitz, *Studies in Bereishis* (Hebrew) 403–07.

55. See Talmud Bavli, Yevamot 65b; *Torah Shelema* [54] and note [54]; Rashi 50:16; Nechama Leibowitz, *Studies in Bereishis* (Hebrew) 403–07.

his sons' concern that Yosef would harm them in retaliation for what they had done to him. According to Rashi, Yaakov did not find it necessary to give this command because "Yosef was not suspected in his eyes."[56] However, as Maharsha notes, Rashi's explanation raises the further question as to why Yaakov and the brothers had different assessments and expectations of Yosef.[57]

Perhaps this episode provides an abiding lesson about the different reactions peers and adults often have toward children on the spectrum. Yosef's brothers remember not only what they did to Yosef, but also Yosef's behaviors as a child that prompted their hatred toward him. Although they have witnessed the remarkable changes he has undergone, they still recall his stubbornly self-centered and self-absorbed behaviors, and they have observed that even in Egypt, Yosef continued to exhibit an obsessive focus on his own dreams and visions, in a way they found both puzzling and disconcerting. They understand, instinctively as well as empirically, that despite the strides he has made and the success he has achieved, Yosef's condition remains a part of him. They know that, like many individuals on the spectrum, he still has trouble letting go, and they fear that he will again revert to behaving like a self-centered *na'ar*; now that he has the opportunity – all these years later – he will finally take revenge.

In contrast, Yaakov may not have appreciated the nature of Yosef's condition or the extent of his deficits, accounting for Yaakov's repeated mistakes in the way he treated Yosef and the way he managed – or mismanaged – Yosef's relationship with his brothers. Likewise, Yaakov did not fully understand the hatred and hostility that Yosef's behaviors prompted in his brothers. Accordingly, Rashi emphasizes that Yosef was not suspected "in [Yaakov's] eyes."[58] Yaakov, an adult, did not see

56. See Rashi 50:16.

57. See Maharsha on Talmud Bavli, Yevamot 65b. This question may be premised on the further assumption that Yaakov was aware of what the brothers had done to Yosef. According to Ramban, Yaakov was not concerned that Yosef would harm his brothers because he never learned that the brothers had harmed Yosef. See Ramban 45:27.

58. See Rashi 50:16.

the qualities in Yosef that caused such disdain among Yosef's peers, and did not realize the degree to which Yosef carried his unpleasant memories of the past with him, still determined to set them right. Thus, in Yaakov's eyes, there was no reason to fear that Yosef would take vengeance on his brothers.

Conclusion

> And Yosef said to them, "Do not fear . . . though you have intended to do me harm, God has intended it for good . . . to allow a large nation to live. And now, do not fear, I will provide for you and your children." And he consoled them and spoke to their heart.[1]

Yosef's thoughtful, gracious, and heartfelt response to his brothers, concluding this episode – and with it, concluding the story of Yosef – may offer a message of optimism for individuals on the spectrum, their families, and their friends. When Yosef's brothers tell him of Yaakov's supposed command that he not take revenge against them, Yosef explains that he has come to terms with what they did, that although they intended to cause him harm, it was all part of God's plan for their success.[2] He assures them that they have no reason to fear, and that he will continue to provide for them and for their children.[3] Though Yosef has previously spoken to his brothers in this way, likewise in an effort to alleviate their guilt and fears, in the past his words have proven less than fully effective, in part because of his seemingly self-serving and self-referential tone.[4]

This time, however, the interaction between Yosef and his brothers is different, because now Yosef is different. Following

1. 50:19–21.
2. 50:19–20.
3. 50:21.
4. Here too, the midrash faults Yosef for stating that "I will provide for you." See *Torah Shelema* [73].

the quotation of Yosef's words to his brothers, the verse concludes with the declaration that Yosef "consoled them and spoke to their heart."[5] The text – perhaps tellingly and, in this reading, fittingly – does not convey the content of Yosef's final words, as the content is not really important. More significantly, the verse emphasizes, Yosef has indeed learned to overcome his condition, to let go of past insults and indignities, to understand others, including his peers, and to talk to them in a manner that shows he relates to them.

Yosef now has the ability to speak to his brothers in a way that can have a real effect on their feelings – finally comforting them – because he now has the ability to see their perspective and to touch their heart. This is now the true Yosef, outside of the trappings of the persona of *Tzafnat Pane'ach,* outside of the protective watch of either Pharaoh or Yaakov, truly reconciled with his brothers. At the conclusion of the story, the reconciliation is complete. Yosef has the confidence to put his trust in his brothers to insure that he is buried in the land that was promised to their fathers.[6]

5. 50:21.
6. 50:24–26.

Published in 2018 by Cavendish Square Publishing, LLC
243 5th Avenue, Suite 136, New York, NY 10016

First Edition

Website: cavendishsq.com

Library of Congress Cataloging-in-Publication Data

Names: Duling, Kaitlyn.
Title: Standing in the Vice President's shoes / Kaitlyn Duling.
Description: New York : Cavendish Square, 2018. | Series: My government | Includes index. | Audience: Grades 2-6.
Identifiers: ISBN 9781502630841 (library bound) | ISBN 9781502630827 (pbk.) | ISBN 9781502630834 (6 pack) | ISBN 9781502630858 (ebook)
Subjects: LCSH: Vice-Presidents--United States--Juvenile literature.
Classification: LCC JK609.5 D85 2018 | DDC 352.23'90973--dc23

Editorial Director: David McNamara
Editor: Jodyanne Benson
Copy Editor: Nathan Heidelberger
Associate Art Director: Amy Greenan
Designer: Jessica Nevins
Production Coordinator: Karol Szymczuk
Photo Research: J8 Media

The photographs in this book are used by permission and through the courtesy of: Cover, White House photo/Wikimedia Commons/File:Old Executive Office Building 1981.jpg; p. 4 ©iStockphoto.com/Lingbeek; p. 6 Pool/Getty Images; p. 8 NurPhoto/Getty Images; p. 9 Chris Maddaloni/CQ-Roll Call Group/Getty Images; p. 10 Xinhua/Alamy; p. 12 The Washington Post/Getty Images; pp. 14, 15 AP Images; p. 16 Alex Wong/Getty Images; p. Kazuhiro Nogi/AFP/Getty Images; p. 18 Bloomberg/Getty Images; p. 20 Mario Tama/Getty Images; p. 21 John Gress/Corbis News/Getty Images; p. 22 Encyclopaedia Britannica/Universal Images Group/Getty Images; p. 24 Ethan Miller/Getty Images; p. 26 Ricky Rycroft/AFP/Getty Images; p. 27 AFP/Getty Images; p. 28 Jose Luis Pelaez Inc/Blend Images/Getty Images.

Printed in the United States of America